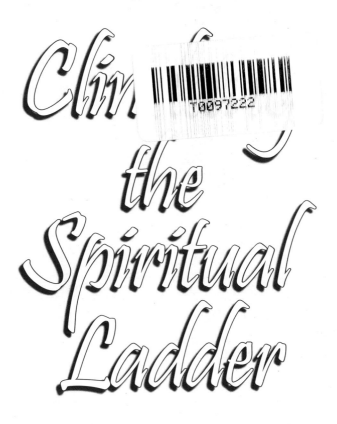

Climbing the Spiritual Ladder

Joan Price, Ph.D.

LOTUS
PRESS

P.O. Box 325
Twin Lakes, Wisconsin 53181 USA

Book Design & Layout: Susan Tinkle

Cover Design and Execution: Susan Tinkle

First Edition 2006

Printed in the United States of America

ISBN 13: 978-0-9409-8589-6
ISBN 10: 0-9409-8589-6

Library of Congress Control Number: 2005938433

LOTUS
PRESS

Published by:
Lotus Press, P.O. Box 325, Twin Lakes, WI 53181 USA
web: www.lotuspress.com
email: lotuspress@lotuspress.com
800.824.6396

Contents

To Fara
Who awakens people to
the goodness of their souls.
I for one am eternally grateful.

Chapter One

The Search

The surfaces of life are easy to understand...
But they do not carry us very far.
They suffice for an active superficial life
from day to day,
But they do not solve the great problems
of existence.

Sri Aurobindo

Born to Search

$\mathcal{M}$ost of us are searching for an answer that will make sense out of our lives. In one way or another most of us have been soul-wounded early in life either by our parents, peers, or society. Such wounds often leave us with injured emotions, a lack of self-esteem, and often afraid to love. Thus we want an answer or answers that give us daily direction, bring us a feeling of peace, and make this complicated world seem more understandable. We want life to be constantly renovated by fresh streams of healing spirit that will give meaning to our activities and soothe our wounds and guilt. Each day we are perpetually reborn, but often we fall into rituals and practices so strictly formulated that they become reruns of old habits, thus lose much, if not all of their interest.

The world today presents a huge kettle of choices for enhancing our spiritual life. Take refuge in meditation retreats, addiction centers, co-dependent groups, transpersonal workshops, and lists of others. Self-help book stacked on self-help book attests to the fact that many are not so comforted by the way we live our lives. We are in a growing group that is restless, feels somehow incomplete, and continues to search. Occasionally we pick up a momentary quick fix: "Health food is the answer" or "Jogging takes the blues away." Yet our soul wounds lie open – unattended. We are often afraid of who we are. We are afraid of being alone. We are afraid of losing the one we love, or of not finding someone to love. We are particularly afraid of being different and therefore rejected.

If only we had the courage to live what the Sufi mystic Jalaluddin Rumi, said: "Conventional knowledge is death to our souls.... Live where you fear to live, destroy your reputation, be notorious." Live the spiritual life.

Actually, everything we do is part of our spiritual life, for we always try to better ourselves in some way. A given system may energize us to go beyond the humdrum of ordinary "conventional knowledge," but any given system has its limitations. And we, in looking outside ourselves for the answer, find only an artificiality that can be overwhelming. Although our activities in the external world are a necessary and even exciting part of our lives, they are only temporary. To become whole and thereby able to close our wounds, we need to become more conscious of our individual uniqueness and integrate it into our everyday lives.

As Henry David Thoreau said, "Go confidently in the direction of your dreams! Live the life you've imagined."

Physical Nature

As with physical nature, our spiritual journey is not a routine and mechanical evolution. Sometimes nature reaches beyond itself even at the cost of sudden retreats. Nature has awe-inspiring sunrises and destructive tornadoes. We know that humans, like nature, may show astounding kindness in the face of diversity and passionately destroy people or nations in the fury of war. Both earth nature and human nature consist of light and darkness or angel and demon. We are intertwined with each other.

The part of nature that people often identify with is the physical, because most of us are involved with our own bodily life. Matter is our foundation – "From dust to dust" reads Genesis – and therefore essential as the basis of our mental and spiritual activities. We belong to this planet, and though all physical matter is in a constant state of change, it is a fit dwelling place for our spiritual journey. According to Hindu philosopher and sage, Aurobindo, spirit is consciousness and "matter is spirit made concrete." Therefore, "all is consciousness." Because the physical world has "the capacity to disclose spiritual and divine content," our physical body is the necessary vehicle of our spiritual life.

If we perceive nature as separate from ourselves, we may have missed the point. Turning away from nature turns us from the completeness of divine wisdom. How can there be a spiritual life that ignores or rejects the importance of the physical body? The soul expresses itself throughout the body in its limbs, organs, nerves, and cells. Thus the body is the temple that pulsates in divine mystery.

True, the physical body and our perception of material things can be obstacles to the spiritual life. If the senses are not satisfied, frustration sets in. Frustration for any length of time may lead to seeking sensuous satisfaction again and again. Physical love, for example, may be short or long lasting, but it is never eternal. And the longer the lover is without physical satisfaction, the more frustration occurs. Such frustration may lead to anger, possessiveness, and even jealousy. In physical love, one person frequently loves the other more than the other person loves him or her. This can lead to more frustration and a greater need to possess and control. Soon we want the other person to begin acting the way we wish him or her to act rather than allowing them to be themselves.

Money, career and worldly success are exclusive and competitive. Other people also want them and must compete to stay ahead. There is always the fear that success could change hands. The thirst for wealth, fame, and power is never satisfied. In Hindu idiom, "To try to extinguish the drive for riches with money is like trying to quench a fire by pouring butter over it." An apt parable might be the donkey driver who kept his donkey moving by dangling before it a carrot tied to a stick that was attached to its own harness. Plato, the great Greek philosopher said, "Poverty consists, not in the decrease of one's possessions, but in the increase of one's greed." The great physicist Stephen W. Hawking confined to a wheelchair his entire life, agreed: "To confine our attention to terrestrial matters would be to limit the human spirit."

One of the major problems with worldly success is self-ishness. We want a beautiful home, a luxury car, and exciting vacations. Many people who reach these goals find their hap-piness short-lived, because none of these attainments survive bodily death. We are not creatures that can be eternally satis-fied with transitory things because we are not limited to the ephemeral realm. Aurobindo taught that conquering worldly desires brings more joy than satisfying them. And he added, "It is for joy and not for sorrow that the world was made." That is why we, like nature, strive for the light.

Myra Richards, known to her students as "The Mother" asked: "Have you never watched a forest with all its countless trees and plants simply struggling to catch the light – twisting and trying in a hundred possible ways just to be in the sun? That is precisely the feeling of aspiration in the physical – the urge, the movement, the push towards the light."

Vital Nature and Emotions

As our physical nature is the temple, emotions are also part of our ultimate fulfillment. If emotions were not part of the divinity, we would not have them. Their relationship to the physical is not clearly defined, but we do know they directly interact with each other. Aurobindo called the higher type of emotion "spiritual passion" or "aspiration." Deep within our soul is passion for the divine, passion for living the spiritual life, and passion for knowledge. Such soul passion may be unconscious or only rear its head upon brief occasions, but it is the vital energy that keeps our spiritual aspirations burning. Unlike spiritual passion, we also have personal emotions that are often bathed in ignorance. Emotional desires can be bru-tal and greedy, driving us toward career, riches, and even empires. By forming attachments to physical objects, people, opinions and organizations, we hope to find security. But worldly desires and pleasures leave us hollow, vacant, and frustrated. "Even earth's sweetest joy is but disguised pain," wrote Drummond. Clinging to the stability of the phenomenal world is like holding on to a bubble for security. On the other hand, emotions may be tender and sensitive tending toward deep compassion and divine love.

Emotions are energy. Passion is energy. We want to avoid killing these vital energies and forcing ourselves into a false quietude. How can we possibly stir up enough vital energy to seek within to know ourselves if we repress emotion? By repressing our emotions (pretending we don't have them), there arises the danger of seeing them revolt one day when we least expect it.

One emotion that many people share is low self-esteem, planted in their psyches at a very early age. Low self-esteem may result in problems such as despondency, addictive behavior, and unforeseen problems in later life. Low self-esteem may manifest as self-hatred, rage, shame, and resentment. People rejected at an early age, for example, often place themselves in a position where they are again rejected. This reinforces their belief that they are not worthy of love. Emotional health is the lifelong job of changing our view of ourselves.

The Mother has said repeatedly that physical health and physical illness alike involve emotional factors. Attacks of illness are attacks of "adverse forces" taking advantage of some weakness in our vital nature. But until we become perfect human beings, illnesses are likely to occur. Although illness may be very distressing, it may also bring us closer to the inner divinity by teaching us to go with the flow of things, especially for those of us who want to be in control of our lives. Illness also may be the gift that teaches us to surrender our ego-driven selves to God.

Tests have shown that individuals interested in the spiritual life are in closer touch with their feelings than most people. Acknowledging our feelings and even sharing them with a friend or family member may be the first step to emotional health. By sharing our deeper emotions, we feel less alienated and alone. On the other hand, suppressing anger or resentment toward other people and toward ourselves may contribute more to illness than to health. Most spiritual teachers suggest that by acknowledging anger and releasing it in some appropriate way, we eventually transform self-destruction into creative energy.

Taking responsibility for our emotional health entails a willingness to feel deeply even when we are afraid. It is always easier to acknowledge our feelings when we feel loved and safe. Once we feel the inner aspiration to take the spiritual path, our associations become a top priority. It is important to choose companions that are loyal, honest, understanding, and moral. This is a safety net, for once we step on the spiritual path, all hell breaks loose. All the negative energy in us rebels against our decision to change our life. The programs (habits, rituals, moods, judgments, etc.) that we have repeated in the past want to continue running. Thus the moment we step on the spiritual path, depression, anger, fear, and doubt do their best to convince us that change is not part of the program. At such times, loyal friends encourage our decision to walk the spiritual path and give us strength to continue the journey.

Taking the spiritual path can be very lonely. We may feel as if we don't fit in with the crowd. With Thoreau, we are hearing the sound of a different drummer. Part of us rejects all the so-called silliness that others enjoy. Another part of us feels rejected. Another part of us wishes we could fit in. Such confusion is often the first sign of growth. A deeper sensitivity to ourselves and to others may be a spiritual message calling us to higher consciousness.

The Mind

The Buddha said, "All that we are is a result of what we have thought." If we speak or act with an evil thought, pain pursues us. If we speak or act with a pure thought, happiness pursues us and never leaves. Such thinking helps us awaken to the recognition that we are mind beings as well as physical and emotional beings. But if we hang on for dear life to familiar concepts (our routine programs), we tend to build iron bars around our minds that keep us from understanding the divine unity of all things. We get trapped in separateness.

We may choose to stay trapped, wounded, and unforgiving, or we may choose to make other choices. The nature of the mental faculty is to think. Though we humans are closely related to the animal, the reasoning mind is our distinguishing feature. Animals are biological creatures ruled mainly by instinct. They, as we, eat, sleep, seek shelter, protect their young, fear loud noises, mark their territory, and use sex for procreation and pleasure. When animals sleep, they dream and when awake they communicate. Higher types of animals such as dolphins, dogs, and apes have developed the ability to reason in practical ways.

If a dog happens to end up on the other side of a fence from his master, he has the capacity to figure out that the best way out of the bind is to retrace his steps to the opening where he went in. Most dogs also have the capacity to draw relationships between events: after a morning walk, my dogs expect a treat. They understand certain words as "walk," which is followed by wagging tails, or "bath," followed by tucked tails.

We humans have higher ability than dogs and dolphins and apes. We have the capacity for abstract reason and beyond. Has a dog, dolphin, or ape ever asked: Who am I? Why am I here? Does life have meaning? What, if anything, is my destiny? Only humans reflect and ponder the relationship between one idea and another idea. Unlike dogs, dolphins, or apes that have no rational moral standards, when our human ability to reason conflicts with our animal desires, we face the problem of *morality*. Most moral choices reflect this internal conflict. For example, when a dog spies a bone in the neighbor's yard, he happily picks it up and carries it home. We don't admonish the dog, "You are an immoral thief!" We know dogs do not make rational moral choices. If, however, we see a pair of binoculars carelessly left in the neighbor's yard and desire to take them with us, the faculty of reason comes into play and a moral conflict arises: "I want the binoculars, but they do not belong to me." Unless the animal desire wins out, we make a moral decision to leave the binoculars where they are.

Most of us are convinced that our mental attitudes, beliefs and thought processes affect our emotional and physical well-being. We live in a time of global communications technology that takes us beyond the thought patterns of our nuclear family, the town newspaper, and traditional religious beliefs. We have the opportunity to transcend early conditioning and choose to accept or reject our parents' values and our cultural mores. Through reflective thought, we can gain autonomy and self-determination, not just by being free from outside pressures, but by consciously choosing goals and values. According to Italian philosopher, Giodano Bruno, "It is proof of a base and low mind for one to wish to think with the masses or majority...Truth does not change because it is, or is not, believed by the majority of people."

As with our emotions, we own a greater freedom if we assume responsibility for our thoughts, beliefs, and values. Reason is a mental faculty that we humans have to help direct our lives. But is the apex of human growth human reason? If so, we should be content to spend our days on the Internet, at the work place dealing with people and numbers, or doing crossword puzzles. These are enjoyable activities, but do any of them give us a feeling of completeness? Reason gives us more freedom than that of the plant or animal led by instinct and limited mental ability, but even the most intellectual human may not reach the inner divinity that gives us peace and wholeness.

Since the beginning of recorded history, we have studied our advances by the development of cities and nations, by the spread of education, by raising housing standards among the poor, by the findings of science towards improved health, ad infinitum. Most of the people who have furthered world progress were creative and disciplined individuals. Look at the poets living among their brilliant visions, the artists absorbed in their art, the philosophers thinking out the problems of the intellect, and the scientists and scholars. These people worked hard and cared deeply for their studies and their experiments, and the work they have contributed to the world is impressive. However, as important as these functions are, can any of them give complete satisfaction? Some of the greatest geniuses the world has known were depressed, suicidal, and cantankerous. Unless the spiritual life is our top priority all of us including the great minds throughout history are yet dissatisfied. Aurobindo found that each of us yearns to develop a higher spiritual consciousness: "The soul wants to go home." If our spiritual nature is the crown of universal existence and matter is its base, then mind and emotions are the link between the two. Spirit is eternal and mind, emotions and matter are its instruments. Aurobindo discovered that spirit needs to be revealed in nature and we are the means to do it.

Higher Consciousness

What is this higher consciousness toward which we strive? Perhaps it is what the world's religions have expressed for centuries. Hinduism calls the higher human consciousness, the true self, Atman – unity with God. Buddhism calls the higher consciousness Nirvana, or the Buddha Nature – ultimate bliss. Christians call the higher consciousness Christ. St. Paul said, "Not I who live, but Christ lives in me." Every religion speaks of the spiritual element within us that, with discipline, surrender, and grace, we could experience. As St. Francis of Assisi so aptly perceived: "What we are looking for is what is looking."

When this higher consciousness – this crowning realization – manifests in our being we become aware of a quickening of the spiritual life. If, as the religions teach, this is the goal of God for us human beings, then we were born to accomplish our right relationship with God and the universe. Yet, we must recognize that as individuals we do not exist in ourselves alone, but in the collectivity of humans, animals, plants, and all material nature. It may be that we as distinct individuals are not the whole sense of God's intention in the world. Now that we know scientifically as well as metaphysically that everything in the world is interrelated, we may feel a strong responsibility not only to ourselves but also to all life everywhere.

Aurobindo and the Mother found that there are as many steps or methods to begin our inner journey to the divinity as there are individuals. If we are inclined toward organized religion, we could use that as a step into our inner spiritual life. Religious rituals have a particular power. We learn by repetition of words, gestures, chants, and participation in sacred ceremonies in a meaningful way. By involvement with the use of mantras or rituals, we connect with history and the people who have practiced it before us. This type of experience could have tremendous force. Each world religion has helped humankind in some way. Paganism increased in people a sense of beauty and appreciation of the sacred in nature. Christianity gave humankind a vision of divine love and charity. Buddhism taught humankind a way to be more compassionate to all sentient beings. Judaism and Islam have shown how to be religiously faithful and zealously devoted to God. Hinduism opened the door to various methods of attaining self-realization. The Mother has said, "A great thing would be done if all these God-visions could embrace and cast themselves into each other."

If our spirituality does not hinge on one particular concept of God or religious observance, we may individually choose to investigate how we relate to ourselves and to others, to the earth and the cosmos. We may look to the fruits of spirituality in the good works of saints and sages or in the work of statespersons and ordinary citizens.

Spiritual leaders have found that most of the methods people choose to attain higher consciousness are founded on the different psychological affinities in our nature. The person of devotion loves a personal God. The seeker of knowledge meditates on the eternal cosmos and its source. The person who wishes to serve aspires to be an instrument of God in the world. Regardless of the method chosen, all spiritual aspirants seek to convert their daily activities and concerns with the world by concentrating them on the Divine.

As we attain greater consciousness in the spiritual life, we discover that love, will-power, and knowledge begin to flow into one another. Love leads to knowledge of the beloved, and to aspiring to become an instrument of the divine. Spiritual knowledge includes love of the divinity, which combined serves all.

Although human beings are one unit, we have two natures. One of our natures is that of ignorance. Ignorance means that we are limited in our knowledge of the divine truth. Ignorance is basically the life of ego – me first. In a group photograph, for example, who do I look for first? Me. That's ego. How many of us want personal recognition when we have done something well? That's ego. Do most of us consider our own bank account more important than the bank account of our neighbor down the street? That's ego. Yet, ego is important. Without it, we would never gain a sense of ourselves as separate and important individuals. Most of us have fairly well developed egos. Ask anyone in the United States to define success and the answer will include wealth and fame. Almost all music, TV, and movies are geared toward satisfying the ego. Are the famous and wealthy any happier than the ordinary person? Why not? The ego, always concerned with "me first" separates us from the Divine. When we realize that ego satisfaction can never make us happy, our conversion from worldly desires to spiritual aspirations begins.

The passage from the life of ego ignorance to the spiritual life does not mean that we must stamp out the ego and never again enjoy life's pleasures. Rather it is a signal to change our ego habits. Instead of living a life where "I am the center of my consciousness," we slowly sense God as the center. Actually, we have unconsciously done this all along. The Divine strength supported us and will continue to support us through all our failings of faith, courage, and patience. The Divine heals the wounds in our soul. With God as our center, we look at the world with new eyes – for God "Makes the blind to see and the lame to stride over the hills."

"Everything you see has its roots in the unseen world,"

said Rumi. "The forms may change, yet the essence remains the same. Every wonderful sight will vanish; every sweet word will fade, but do not be disheartened, the source they come from is eternal, growing, branching out giving new life and new joy. Why do you weep? The source is within you and this whole world is springing up from it."

In the words of Aurobindo: "Find out thy soul, recover thy hid self, in silence seek god's meaning in thy depths."

Chapter Two

Ego & the Roles We Play

Every action of man is full of ego –
 the good ones as well as the bad,
 his humility as much as his pride,
 his virtues as much as his vices.

Sri Aurobindo

The Ego

*O*ne of the first steps in knowing who we are is to understand that puzzling characteristic of our soul personality called the *ego*. In contemporary Western tradition, the first individual to examine the workings of the ego in some depth was Sigmund Freud. For him, the psyche is the seat of both our mind and our passions, and like other Eastern and Western systems, Freud said the psyche was tripartite. For him the psyche includes 1) the *id* – unconscious drives that sometimes take over, 2) the *ego* – the self-conscious "I," and 3) the *super-ego* – which is critical of the ego and enforces moral standards on it.

In the early days Freud's notions of infantile sexuality shocked the world, especially the idea that a male child desired his mother sexually and hated his father as a rival. The *Kabala*, an important mystical writing belonging to the Jewish religion, disagreed with Freud. According to *Kabala*, babies are not merely biological and sexual, but have a soul that reacts to the past-life relationship it may have had with the family it has been born into. Therefore, past-life experiences (See Ch. 7) have a profound effect upon the formation of the ego and its attitude towards male and female.

The *Kabala* is saying that based on our experiences and choices in past lives, we choose the parents in this life that can best give us the soul experiences we need for spiritual advancement toward knowing ourselves. In other words, the family our soul chooses (unknown to our conscious ego) is an important factor in our spiritual growth. Love, pain and pleasure, joy and sorrow, are all necessary attributes that lead to spiritual maturity.

With Freud, the Swiss psychoanalyst Dr. Carl G. Jung discovered that we have both a *conscious* and an *unconscious* level of being. For Jung, the ego is the center of consciousness and the seat of our individual identity. Everything in our conscious life is connected to the ego, such as going to movies, communicating with friends, and choosing careers. In the unconscious lie the answers to our deepest eternal questions: "Who am I?" "Why am I here?" "What is the destiny of humankind?"

As opposed to many Eastern traditions that consider the ego inferior and something to eliminate, Western traditions view the ego as the foundation of the soul and encourage it to perform well. The job of the ego is to maintain our relationship with the world with emphasis on our personal wants and needs. With the ego we make everyday choices, but sometimes, when our choices come from the unconscious, the ego is at a loss. How often have we asked ourselves, "Why me?" "What did I do to deserve this?"

The Hindu saint Ramakrishna answered the question, "Why me?" using the metaphor of cards. He said that we are dealt a hand of cards based on the thoughts and deeds we had in a past life or lives. We cannot choose different cards, but we can in this life choose how to play the hand we hold. He said it would be impractical to deny our cards or to wish that our cards were different from what they are – that we had different parents, a different face, were of another race or sex. These reactions, though tempting, are a waste of effort and lead nowhere. The idea, he said, is to play the cards to the best of our ability.

The ego plays the cards. It chooses, denies, accepts or rejects. But the ego doesn't know the game. The *whys* of the game lie hidden in the unconscious, in the laws of the universe, or what Aurobindo called the Truth-Consciousness. The purpose of life is to grow out of our ego-ignorance into self-knowledge. With more self-knowledge we would play the cards differently.

Personal Identity

Everything in our conscious life is connected to the ego. According to Aurobindo, "Human nature is shot through in all its stuff with the thread of the ego; even when one tries to get away from it, it is in front or could be behind all the thoughts and actions like a shadow." Through the ego, we see ourselves as separate from each other and from all things in the world. Though mystics and quantum physicists perceive everything in the world as interrelated, the ego sees itself divided from the rest of the world. It operates in terms of subject and object: I versus You and We versus They. Ego always considers itself more important than anything or anyone else. How many of us are more interested in the amount of our own paycheck than whether our neighbor got a raise? How many are more concerned with food for their own loved ones than for the homeless? We are happy that we were invited to a party and depressed if we weren't. We wish we had a Mercedes instead of a Ford. That's ego! Ego represents our *personal identity.*

As egoistic persons, we want to feel superior to others in some way. For example, think of someone you don't like. Now imagine that you hear negative gossip about that person. Are you secretly pleased? Let's imagine further that you find out the gossip is false. Are you disappointed? This illustrates our desire to feel superior to others. It also happens with people we like. When a friend initially receives honors, we are glad, but if the honors continue to pile up, we get defensive. The ego in us wants to be recognized as well. Recall the group photograph. We look first to see how our face comes through before turning attention to the picture as a whole. We may campaign for the poor, but where is the person who gives the poor his or her own pay raise? The more concerned we are with our own welfare, the less compassion we have for the rest of life. The Buddha said the less compassion we have for others, the greater our suffering.

Egoism is always involved with vanity, pride, and self-esteem and is therefore not very levelheaded. One day I may feel good about myself, and the next day I may feel bad about myself. Ego swings from the exuberance of feeling great to the depression of feeling awful. We want to feel like we are someone special and we often succeed, but then we swing in the opposite direction and feel like we are nobody at all – a total failure. The ego is fascinating. In the course of a day we can praise ourselves one minute and condemn ourselves the next minute. Watch yourself especially if alone and doing something around the house. See what happens if you drop something or burn the toast.

Ego humor has the ability to touch our unconscious by revealing the sense of the ridiculous. Charlie Chaplin's comic persona was very much that of the rich dandy who was actually a poor hobo. *The Secret Life of Walter Mitty* is the story about a meek clerk with inner fantasies of being a dashing hero. We laugh at matters that affect us deeply, because they reveal a familiar shared ache.

The Conscious and the Unconscious

Jung called the inner world the realm of the unconscious because we are not conscious of its contents. The realm of the unconscious includes everything outside our conscious awareness that is not connected with ego. The ego stands between our inner world and outer world and can adapt to both, but the inner world has much more influence on our lives than we realize. Jung discovered that our primitive instincts and our deep desires such as sex and feelings of love are instincts from the unconscious. If the ego doesn't check these strong instinctive drives, biological nature may take over our lives and cause us big trouble. The ego helps out, not in choosing our feeling of love, but how we handle our actions.

The ego accepts or rejects judgments of our family and of society, especially in judgments of right and wrong. These ego attitudes develop throughout our lives. Our parents try to communicate their moral standards by rewarding us for fulfilling them. If they reward us for being neat and tidy, then neatness will probably become one of our values, and we may condemn those who are not neat and tidy. In that way we integrate our parents' morality into our own behavior, because by gaining their approval, we avoid their disapproval. If our parents consider neatness a virtue and punish us for getting dirty, then dirtiness becomes something bad.

The Masks We Wear

Looking to the early Greek dramatists, Jung called the roles we play the *persona*. The persona is a "mask" we wear both to impress others and to conceal our true nature. On certain occasions, when we feel the need to strike a compromise between our own individuality and social expectations, we conform by wearing a mask or *false face*. The persona is a compromise between ourselves as we really are and society – a protective covering that shields our deeply personal, intimate, and vulnerable self from the public. The persona allows us to endure people we don't like and to attain personal achievement.

We may wear many masks: businessperson, student, professor, computer programmer, banker, artist, interior designer, and so on. Have you ever wanted to tell a colleague exactly how you felt, but said nothing? Have you ever come home from work dead tired and want nothing more than to go in the house, kick off your shoes and relax, when your neighbor gives you a fifteen minute critique on the new developments of child rearing? To show consideration, you play the role of concerned neighbor and friend. Or in the morning when the only thing you want is peace and quiet while your companion talks incessantly and you pretend to be the interested listener.

Clothes too are part of our persona. People judge others by their clothes and if we don't dress properly we are considered unreliable. The president of the United States does not wear hiking shorts and boots while giving a news conference.

Ministers and priests do not wear bathing suits while serving at the altar, and professors seldom lecture a class in bare feet. We wear bathing suits on the beach, put on business clothes for work, and don a suitable outfit to social affairs. There are exceptions: Parents may wear pajamas and robe while driving their children to school, praying all the while that they don't have an automobile accident.

Society expects each of us to play the part we are assigned as perfectly as possible. If you are a checkout person at a market, your employer expects you to be cheerful and tell each customer to have a nice day. If you are a doctor, patients expect you to wear a clean white frock. An artist however could wear sneakers, a tee shirt, and jeans. A doctor wearing such an outfit would be suspect, as would the Queen of England wearing a softball uniform with cap and cleats at a cocktail party.

In a professional situation, playing a role may include our attitude and relations with superiors – our political opinion, the neighborhood we live in, the car we drive, even our choice of partners. The masks we wear indicate that if we play our cards right, we will win the game. By not playing the role of industrious worker, responsible citizen, dependable in all that we do, the boss may pass us over for advancement or we may be out of a job.

Language is also an important part of our role. We expect educators to use correct grammar and if they don't we question their reliability. But we do not question the reliability of a motorcycle mechanic if poor grammar is spoken so long as that person has the expertise to fix the motorcycle. When others do not use the language structure we prefer, we often wear the mask of interest, which is a way of showing consideration, when actually we aren't very interested in what they are saying.

After work, at home, we feel freer to remove the mask. Our partner knows us as we really are. At home we can say with some confidence, "I'm busy, I'll help in a minute," or "I'd rather read than watch TV tonight." However, some people play their roles even at home: the teacher continues to lecture, the boss tells his or her mate exactly what to do, the engineer insists on precision. Those who identify with their public mask are in jeopardy of losing their self-identity. We must be able to put these personas away when we are through with them.

When some individuals remove the mask, however, they uncover their unconscious primitive side. The minister, kind and caring to the public, kicks the dog and swears at his or her companion. The work-alcoholic executive slumps down on the sofa and doesn't lift a finger to help. As we progress in knowing ourselves, we become more conscious of the masks we wear. Our true nature has no masks. It is objective and never dismayed by anything. To release the true self, we must gradually stop playing all the unnecessary roles. And when we do choose a role to play, it is important to be very conscious of the choice we made and why we made it. The Dalai Lama said, "I don't think a person should have two sides. There should be no gap, that is not honest."

The Shadow

Beneath our masks and much deeper than the ego, lies the shadowy unconscious in each of us. The shadow is the part of ourselves that we repress from our consciousness because we don't want to see it as part of our self-image. It usually contains inferior qualities and weaknesses that the ego refuses to recognize. As a result we *project* our shadow onto other people. When we project our unacceptable qualities on others, we are able to hate and condemn freely the weakness and evil we see in them and still maintain our own sense of righteousness. The shadow may be positive or negative. We may project our "positive" shadow on others by building them up and tearing ourselves down: "She has so much talent and I have none."

Here's a test to discover your own shadow. Think of three traits in other people that you dislike the most – not that you just slightly dislike, but things that upset you emotionally. These traits could be anything – dishonesty, showing off, gossip, bigots, hypocrites, prejudices, and so on. Are you ready for a shock? These same traits that repulse us in others are traits hidden within us that we refuse to admit we possess. We have repressed them, because we do not like them and refuse to admit them. But Jung believed if these characteristics were not in us, we could not recognize them in others. As Mahatma Gandhi said, "How could I recognize evil in others if I did not have it in myself?" Evil would have no meaning. That may be why Jesus preached to remove the beam in our own eye before we tried to remove it from another.

Projection means the qualities that we most dislike in another person could in most cases give us a description of our own unconscious negative side. We may abhor dishonesty in others and refuse to see any dishonesty in ourselves. But if we take a deeper look we may see that we tell "little white lies" to protect ourselves from embarrassment. And we add to the lie by convincing ourselves that we told the "little white lie" to protect the other person. How often are we dishonest with ourselves about our motives? Do you ever promise yourself that you will get your work done after watching TV for only fifteen minutes? Two hours later you're still watching TV.

Projections are always bound up in emotion. Jung said we are unconsciously tied to that to which we are blind. If we refuse to admit we have the same qualities we strongly dislike in others, we are bound to those very qualities. When we realize that our powerful dislikes reside in our own being, we can then free ourselves of them. For instance, if I refuse to admit to myself that I have any capacity for anger, the anger buried in my unconscious (shadow) could erupt and take me over when I least expect it.

Imagine that you are introduced to a small group of people and after having conversed only a short while, you have an intense dislike for a total stranger – too pushy, too abrasive, too critical. To the extent that you are willing to see it, this immediate dislike is a projection of something in yourself that you are unwilling to accept. You see your own negative qualities in the other person while not being able to see those same qualities in yourself.

An example lies in a story about the Buddha:

An angry man, learning that the Buddha observed the principle of great love that com-
mends the return of good for evil, came and
verbally abused him. The Buddha was silent,
pitying his folly. When the man had finished
his abuse, the Buddha asked him, "Son, if a
man declined to accept a present made to
him, to who would the present belong?" The
angry man answered, "In that case it would
belong to the man who offered it." "My son,"
said the Buddha, "I decline to accept your
abuse, and request you to keep it yourself...
A wicked man who reproaches a virtuous one
is like one who looks up and spits at heaven;
the spit soils not the heaven, but comes back
and defiles his own person."

The abuser went away ashamed, but he
came again and took refuge in the Buddha.

When the Buddha refused to accept the verbal abuse, he
was refusing to accept the angry man's projection. An important point is the Buddha offered pure love and compassion
for the angry man. We cannot pretend to refuse a projection
while inside ourselves we are experiencing strong negative
emotion. We must be honest.

Jung said we accept the moral parts of ourselves – that we
feed the hungry, forgive an insult, and love our enemy in the
name of Christ. These are valuable virtues, but we need also
to look deeper and discover the beggar, the thief, the of-
fender, and the hypocrite within ourselves. We must learn
that I myself am the enemy who must be loved. Yet, there is
another side of the shadow from which all *inspirations* come.
When we plunge into creative activities, the ego and the
shadow actually work together. Rather than obstructing instinctive forces, the ego channels them. At such times, our
consciousness expands and we feel full of life and vigor.

The problem of the shadow and its projection applies to
collective society as well as the individual. The persecution of

the Jews by the Nazis is an example of the extent to which a collective shadow projection can go. Prejudice and discrimination against minority groups, religious beliefs, and alternative lifestyles are all projections of the collective shadow.

Jung realized that neither *choice* nor *will* could function when we are unconscious. No matter how painful the experience, we must recognize the shadow. One of the better ways to check our own shadow is by paying attention to what makes us angry in other people. We may also suspect our shadow at the amount of satisfaction we feel at other people's weaknesses. Their failings heighten our feelings of virtuosity.

We cannot recognize the shadow until we are face to face with another person onto whom we project it. Then suddenly we realize our projection. In a flash, we see that it isn't their temper or selfishness, but our own temper or selfish thoughtlessness that is so bothersome. From the moment of recognition we begin to walk toward freedom.

Trust

Acknowledging who we are is a bold venture. From the beginning of our awareness that we are unique individuals and not members of the "herd," we feel isolation – there is no more comforting word for it. I doubt if there is a human being who has not felt isolation of some sort. Neither family nor society nor position can save us from this fate, or the most successful adaptation to our environment, however smoothly we play the role. The development of our personality, if we are to be true to ourselves, is something that must be paid for dearly.

The unfolding of personality means to trust the law of our own being. We must develop a loyal perseverance and confident hope by choosing our own way, consciously and with moral deliberation. But we only can make a moral decision to go our own way if we trust ourselves. If we are convinced that another way is better, we might play that role instead of striking out on our own. We may even accept and try to follow the conventional moral, political, and religious views of society. But following the crowd is not the ideal, either morally or spiritually. The thoughts and actions of the masses or herd are merely the echoes of the collective thinking of the society in which we live. Society projects its dark side on other nations, political parties, religions, and unique individuals. Submission to the common denominator always means renouncing our wholeness and running away from the consequences of our own being. Recall the remarks of poet Jalaluddin Rumi: "Conventional knowledge is death to our souls... Live where you fear to live, destroy your reputation, be notorious." Live the spiritual life.

Follow Your Bliss

To develop our individuality is an unpopular undertaking in society. Some people have accomplished their individuality to some extent, but only a few individuals have accomplished it completely – Jesus, Moses, Buddha, Mohammad, Aurobindo, Socrates, Plato – sages, saints, and warriors. They are the heroes. Their greatness has never been in their submission to convention, but in their unique individuality. They towered like mountain peaks above the masses that still clung to the herd mentality. Heroes are not always public figures, however. As mythologist Joseph Campbell said, anyone who has the courage to follow his or her bliss is a hero.

If we refuse to listen to the inner voice, we may miss our spiritual calling. To the extent that we are untrue to the law of our being and do not rise to the challenge, we could fail to realize our life's meaning. Some people never question the meaning of their lives therefore they don't seek an answer. But if we are to live more fully and consciously, it is of utmost importance to increase our awareness.

The Hero

In myths throughout the ages, the hero's birth and life are always threatened. The serpents sent by Hera to destroy the infant Hercules, the python that tries to strangle Apollo at birth, the massacre of the innocents – all these tell a story similar to what you and I have experienced.

Like the myths, we search for balance and clarity. We adjust, making events somehow correspond to the inner necessity of things. It is this tension between the black and white, good and evil, positive and negative, active and passive, that gives the myths (and our lives) their power.

So what in us corresponds to the hero? None of us is Achilles, or a Lancelot, King Arthur, Ulysses, Isis or Persephone. And yet, don't we partake of all those characters? We too must slay the inner dragons. We too must journey to our own dark underworld and rescue the imprisoned princess or prince. As P.L Travers said, "Everybody has to be the hero of one story: his [her] own." Our homeland is well described in *Rumpelistiltskin*: "The country where the fox and the hare say goodnight to each other." This is the "Promised Land" where all opposites are reconciled – the land where we go beyond ego to discover our true self.

What must we do to arrive at the "Promised Land"? First we must feel the need to transform our ego desires and self-ishness. Negative feelings such as anger, jealously, anxiety and stress are always painful experiences that warn us something is wrong. If we are aware of pain, we are on the first leg of the journey. Why? We no longer deny that we are suffering. Second, we need to look at ourselves. What are our strengths? What are our weaknesses? What habits do we like and what habits would we like to change? We need to take a look at our responses. Are we blaming the external world for our difficulties? If so, then we need to turn our attention within. As the Dalai Lama said, "If we expect all our problems to be solved by external means, that is a mistake." The world is our projection. If we are in love, the world is beautiful. If we are suffering, the world is ugly. Both of these attitudes come from within, so we might want to pay more attention to our attitudes. Philosopher William James wrote: "The greatest discovery of my generation is that a human being can alter his life by altering his attitude." Third, we need to step out of the ego into the spiritual life. Spiritual principles are beyond the level of ego. Ego desires change constantly – Truth is changeless. Inner peace develops to the same extent that we immerse ourselves in the spiritual life. Inner peace is filled with joy, because it is truth and *the truth shall make us free.*

In the words of Aurobindo, "The remedy is to think constantly of the Divine, not of oneself, to work, to act, do sadhana [spiritual practice] for the Divine; not to consider how this or that affects *me* personally, not to claim anything, but to refer all to the Divine."

Chapter Three

The Balance Within

*Creative, spiritually productive people
are usually those with a large share of
contra sexual features.*

Carl G. Jung

Masculine and Feminine

*T*hroughout the history of the human race, men and women have had certain stereotypical roles to play. Generally, the "real man" was powerful, competitive, objective, the provider and decision-maker. The "true woman" bore children, nurtured the family, cooked, cleaned, sewed, and supported her husband emotionally. Both men and women were destined to this role whether or not they wished to, or were particularly gifted to do so. Men who shed tears were weak. Women who pursued professional careers were suspect. The polarization was safe as long as the men, women, and their children played their roles.

Until recently, people projected their views of masculine and feminine role-playing on everything:

Science . .. . masculine
The Arts .. .. feminine
Sports .. .. masculine
Homemaker .. .. feminine
Reason . .. . masculine
Intuition .. .. feminine
Objective .. .. masculine
Subjective .. .. feminine
Spirit . .. . masculine
Matter .. .. feminine

YIN/YANG

Today, we realize the 'masculine' and 'feminine' qualities co-exist in each human being and in everything in the universe. No one is altogether masculine or exclusively feminine. For example, a symbol of the balance of these qualities in Chinese Taoist philosophy is the *yin/yang.*

Feminine  Masculine

Based on keen observations of nature, humans, and the heavens, Chinese Taoist philosophers recognized the interaction of two opposing principles known as *yin* (the "dark side") and *yang* (the "light side"). Note that both the *yin* and *yang* are included within the circle. Neither one can exist without the other. Without the *yin, yang* is unmanifest. Without *yang, yin* cannot manifest. Together *yin* and *yang* produce the universe. The *yin* principle is fertile, mysterious, secret, and female. It predominates in all that is cool, moist, dark, or passive. The *yang* principle is found in the sun and in fire. It is male and has to do with all that is hot, dry, bright, or active.

An example of how the *yin* and the *yang* work together can be found in the ordinary electrical plug and wall socket. Electricians call the plug male and the wall socket female. Alone they produce nothing. When the plug enters the wall socket, electricity flows. Although the example of the plug and wall socket is physical, the *yin* and *yang* symbolize the psychological and spiritual as well. A man that is sensitive to his surroundings and other people's feelings is balancing his *yang* with the *yin.* A woman that makes logical and objective decisions is affirming the *yang* in her life.

If we bring everything into balance by marrying the opposites within us, we establish a real balance between *yin* and *yang*. And out of that real and mysterious balance a new order, a new insight and love is born in each of us in the very ground of our being that is beyond all role playing. This insight and love is the fountain of the spiritual life.

To the Taoists, the *yang* is not superior to the *yin*, nor is the *yin* superior to the *yang,* because each is present in the other and both exist in balance to produce the "way of nature." Heaven is *yang* and nature is *yin*. Humans contain elements of both heaven and nature: and though males are predominantly *yang* and females predominantly *yin*, each principle reveals characteristics of the other. Jung believed that spiritual people must have a balance of *yin* and *yang* to be whole and complete human beings. Some philosophers and scientists today believe that as we humans evolve spiritually, we will become androgynous – a harmonious balance of *yin/yang* – feminine/masculine.

Eastern Views

The idea of balance between the masculine and feminine aspects is not limited to the Chinese Taoist principle of *yin/yang*. *The Tibetan Book of the Dead* calls for us to meditate upon the Father-Mother Guru. Upon seeking rebirth the person experiencing the afterlife states is told: "When you see them (the Father-Mother Guru), remember to withhold yourself from going between them." This implies there is a union in the soul of each individual, and it is important to recognize this union. In Hindu mythology, the gods and goddesses perform as a unit. Together they create, preserve, and destroy the world. Brahma with his spouse Saraswati creates the world. Vishnu and his companion Lakshmi preserve the world until it gets out of balance. Then Shiva and his cohort Shakti destroy the disorder and the cycle continues.

Western Views

In the Western traditions – Judaism, Christianity, and Islam –

we have Adam and Eve, the masculine and feminine in the Garden of Bliss. Unlike the Eastern traditions, the Western traditions devalued the spiritual significance of the feminine. First, they only worshipped a male god: Yahweh, the "jealous God" would have no other gods before him. Nor did Yahweh mention the possibility of a female consort who might have a share in his power. Second, they viewed the feminine (Eve) as evil. The Genesis 2 Adam and Eve story was the beginning of strict separation between the masculine and feminine roles in the Western world. In Genesis 2: 18-22, which is the most widely acclaimed Adam and Eve myth, God fashioned man (Adam) in his own image. As an after thought, he fashioned Eve from Adam's rib to be his helpmate. This powerful character of Yahweh provided the prototype for the dominant male. But in so doing, the balance of masculine and feminine power was left afloat. Thus, from the beginning of Western culture, women were considered inferior, even suspect. To make matters worse, Eve talked Adam into eating the apple of the tree of knowledge.

There is, however, a less popular and seldom talked about account in the creation story of Adam and Eve. The Genesis 2 myth established the primacy of the male and the inferiority of the female. But in Genesis 1: 27-28, we find another version, an even older version, in which man and woman are created together: "So God created man in His own image, in the image of God created He him: *male and female created He them*" (italics mine). Here we have God containing masculine and feminine characteristics similar to the *yin/yang* and empowering humankind (made in God's image) with a balance. That is not to say that women are also men or that men are also women. What it clearly says to me is women and men are coequal, not one-sided beings who will always be seduced by, but never really understand the other.

A Healthy Balance

Marion Woodman has said that a much needed balance between the masculine and feminine will mark the next stage of our evolution. In the Western world, we have repressed an important aspect of our feminine nature. Patriarchal power structures have driven the feminine nature into obscurity. Woodman said the reason for suppressing the feminine is fear. In patriarchies, she said, healthy masculine energy becomes "distorted into a rigid worship of logic, control, and machine-like perfection."

As we know, patriarchies expect women to display the feminine qualities of love, nurturing, and purity. But they do not want the dark side of the feminine to reveal itself. The feminine shadow is associated with the body, birth, life, blood, and death. Patriarchies want to rise above the feminine because they are afraid to surrender to nature, to emotion, the unconscious, and death. But without surrender, there can be no creativity, no intuition, or life. Real life is possible only to those who are open to change, to creativity, and to death, even daily death of our emotions, mind, and body.

Women that accept patriarch rule are also afraid. By allowing men to control their lives in business, religion, and at home, women avoid taking responsibility for their own lives. They do not have to make logical and objective decisions, because the men take care of it. Such women do not want the dark side of masculinity as rigidity and expectations of perfection to reveal itself. However, there is the healthy masculine that has direction, focus, discernment, discrimination, and creative power.

Jung said that a man automatically projects the feminine aspects of his soul outside of himself onto a woman. That woman will carry the feminine aspect for the man and he won't have to deal with it. A woman will project the masculine aspects of herself onto a male, thus saving her the trouble of becoming conscious of the masculine within her soul. As soon as we commit to the spiritual path, however, the opposite begins to occur. The spiritual man no longer projects the feminine aspects of his soul onto a female, rather he assimilates the feminine aspect within himself. And the spiritual woman does not project the masculine part of her soul onto a male – she works on the inner fusion of male and female within herself. The lack of projecting the opposite principle onto someone else makes people on the spiritual path uniquely attuned to the balance within – androgyny – "holy androgyny."

Because spiritual people tend to project less onto the opposite sex, they more easily attune to the balance within. They become the living presence of the non-dual, male-female character of the divine. This gives them an incredible access to the spiritual life. Two examples of the masculine and feminine balance in highly spiritual people are Joan of Arc and St. Francis of Assisi. Joan of Arc transcended the stereotypical feminine qualities by resolutely following the inner angelic voice that guided her to help conquer armies. St. Francis personified love, gentleness, and caring as well as the qualities of leadership. As Aurobindo told his disciples over again: "The Mother's consciousness and my consciousness are one."

Androgyny

Throughout the ages, the spiritual traditions have asserted that the inner being of each of us, that toward which all spiritual paths lead, is androgynous. So, what exactly is androgyny? The path leading toward androgyny is a path toward wholeness. Androgyny is the balance and interrelating of male and female aspects of the psyche. We could say androgyny is the *asexual* nature of our soul. It is the innermost part of us that we truly are. Androgyny is the ability to attain an inner fusion of the male and female components of the being so that we blossom into full spiritual power. "The truth is," said Samuel Coleridge, "a great mind must be androgynous."

Androgyny is not a matter of neutralizing the masculine and feminine qualities, but of reconciling them in an inner mystical marriage. Jung recognized the need for such integration of our own inner male and female aspects if we were to become spiritual persons. He certainly was not saying that our body changes, but to the extent that our faculties of feeling, thinking, intuition, and sensing are developed – to that degree the ego identifies with the body. For example, at the extreme of maleness we have the big, dumb, macho muscleman. At the extreme of femaleness, we have the bubble-headed blond with sensuous bosom and curves. These stereotypes represent individuals who have an extreme one-sided development.

As the other qualities of our personalities develop, the ego becomes less and less tied to the body type. We usually consider *thinking* to be a male faculty and *feeling* a female faculty. But in the androgynous person both faculties would be highly developed as would intuition and sensing abilities. By integrating these faculties, we expand our capacity for spiritual experience. However, in most of us certain faculties predominate.

Rising to the spiritual level of consciousness, a woman accepts continuous enrichment from her masculine side by living it out in the external world. She makes decisions, thinks clearly, and determines her own values. A man who has freed himself of the role-playing personas incubates the seeds of his creativity in the dark mysterious depths of his own soul. He is aware of deep feelings, is able to establish friendships, and show unlimited compassion to others in need. And the more we are able to unite the masculine and feminine qualities within ourselves, the greater potential to live spiritual lives. We must, of course be careful not to overdo the "otherness" in ourselves by denying our own natural femininity or masculinity. We are looking for balance – androgyny.

In the spiritual life, the balance consists of a partnership within our self. An example of a balanced individual was Jesus the Christ. According to the New Testament gospels, Jesus was a man-god/god-man whose masculine power and leadership blended perfectly with his inspired feminine love and warmth. He knocked over the tables of the moneychangers and chased them out of the temple. He forgave his enemies and loved those that persecuted him. If what we read is correct, Jesus was completely balanced and he said that we could become the same: "As I am so can you be."

Androgyny calls us to reach higher than identifying with

our sexuality. We must integrate the masculine and feminine energies. Like *yin* and *yang,* our souls need to unite the masculine and feminine for full enlightenment.

As Jesus said in the Gospel of Saint Thomas:

> When you make the male and the female
> into a single one, so that the male will
> not be male and the female not be female...
> then you will enter the Kingdom.

Chapter Four

Training for the
Spiritual Life

*Concentration and will can be developed
as well as muscles; they grow by regular
training and exercise.*

Myra Richards (The Mother)

The Eightfold Path

*T*he Buddha believed that we must train for spiritual life just as intentionally as we train for athletic achievement or for our profession. First, we should associate with wise and truthful people, converse with them, observe their ways, and assimilate their spirit of love and compassion. Next, he taught that "intentional living" could best be learned by following the Eightfold Path: *1) Right views, 2) Right aspiration, 3) Right speech, 4) Right conduct, 5) Right occupation, 6) Right effort, 7) Right attention, 8) Right concentration.*

1) *Right views.* Unselfish motivation brings joy: selfish desire brings pain. The beginning of wisdom is to understand life's problem.

2) *Right aspiration.* Right aspiration is the wisdom to free us from selfish desires, ill will, and violence. Right aspiration is cultivating compassion for all suffering beings and feeling joy in the success and happiness of others. Sincerity is the key.

3) *Right speech.* Language is a sign of our character. Avoid all talk that will lead to unhappiness and use speech to bring about happiness. A

person who speaks the truth is worthy of trust. One who repeats gossip causes dissension.

4) *Right conduct.* Our actions should promote peace and happiness for others and we should show respect for the well being of all sentient creatures.

5) *Right occupation.* Choose an occupation that brings good to others. Avoid occupations that harm people, animals, the environment, or violate the moral law within.

6) *Right effort.* The Buddha stressed the importance of using good will to discipline the mind. Disciplined good will helps direct our thoughts to compassion and unselfishness.

7) *Right attention.* Keep the mind centered. Meditate on the goal. Practice attention while walking, sitting, eating, or talking. Become aware of the interconnectedness of everything in the universe.

8) *Right concentration.* (Quieting the mind). The last and important stage of the Eightfold Path is the culmination of right effort and right attention. This is the level of sainthood.

Following the Eightfold Path is a difficult task. It takes immense patience, persistence, and personal effort. We may do well some days and lousy other days. It is important not to condemn ourselves if we fall off the path. Patience is very important. Each person may interpret the meaning of the steps differently, but eventually there will intervene an uplifting of our knowledge and effort from our ordinary views to spiritual experience. We could experience a direct suggestion from within ourselves. The Buddha said to listen closely – the inner voice will be your teacher. The amount of time it takes to change our attitude is less important than we may think. Recall the Hindu saying: "God is not in a hurry."

The Divine Touch

According to the living traditions, the supreme spirit is in the heart of every thinking and living being. It is like a rose bud closed and folded up within us. It opens swiftly or gradually, petal-by-petal, once we begin to turn our minds and hearts toward the divine. Our disciplined lives and thoughts begin to remove the obstacles that block our way to the spiritual life. The Mother said, "Those who choose God have been chosen by God." The divine touch awakens and opens the spirit. Once we receive the touch, we will attain an interrelationship and eventually unity with God, whether in the course of one human life or through many incarnations.

Sages have discovered that nothing can be taught to our soul that is not already potentially in the soul. Thus all the spiritual knowledge we are capable of attaining is only realizing the spirit within us. Remember the woman that touched the hem of Jesus' garment? When he felt her touch, he said, "Your faith [in Christ] has healed you." We can know the divine and become the divine because we are already that in our soul. "Is it not written in your law, 'I have said, you are gods'?" (NT: John 10:34). Socrates and Plato agreed that all spiritual teaching reveals what we already know but don't realize that we know.

An important start in our spiritual training is to recognize that we do not consciously know the depths of the spiritual life. When living the egoistic life, we often think we know the truth, but do not know the truth. All we have are opinions. "The opinionated person," said Aurobindo, "is usually without knowledge." In the words of the scientist Copernicus, "To know that we know what we know, and to know that we do not know what we do not know, that is true knowledge." Knowledgeable people listen to alternative ways of looking at human nature, the universe, and God – always aspiring to learn. We could say the undisciplined person floats on shallow waters. The disciplined person dives into deep waters. But we must not dive into deep waters until we learn how to swim. Aurobindo suggested three aids to help us learn how to swim: 1) the word, 2) personal effort, and 3) to establish contact with God.

The Word

According to Aurobindo, the first important aid in our training for spiritual truth is the *Word* – that which is heard. The word may come to us from within (the inner voice) or it may come to us from outside (from a teacher or book). In either case, the word is an instrument for setting hidden knowledge to work. The word within may be the voice of the soul in us that is always open to the divine, or it may be the word of the "Divine Master" that dwells in the hearts of all. Most of us need the guidance of the word from outside ourselves – from a book or a teacher. The *Bible,* the *Koran,* the *Diamond Sutra,* the *Bhagavad-Gita,* or any scripture may light a spark in us – an awakening or a sudden realization. Also, the instructions of a spiritual teacher may inspire us to step on the spiritual path. But that is in the beginning and the beginning may last twenty years or two hundred lifetimes. In the end, we must experience the divine truth, beauty, and goodness in our own soul beyond the written or spoken truth.

Take the word *love.* No matter how much we read or hear about love, we cannot actually understand the meaning until we experience love for ourselves. We read love poems and feel their beauty, but only when we fall romantically in love do we have the "Aha" experience. Only as we move deeper into the love of friendship, then into love of the universe and God, do we begin to understand the nature of spiritual love.

Tradition and scripture could be important tools for living the spiritual life, because they embrace the knowledge received from the past and also contain certain eternal truths. But often these thoughts are written in unfamiliar terms that no longer apply to our generation. As our forefathers and mothers had to grapple with terms they could understand, we need to adapt these universal truths into new terms that fit our lives today.

Each religion has been formed to help guide the thoughts and practices of their congregations. They have taken as much as possible from universal truths and principles then developed a fixed system that its members must follow. These routines and rituals may be an important aid and guide if we use them as signposts to point us in the right direction. Spirituality may be found everywhere, not only in temples, churches, and synagogues, not only in the stars, not only in music and song and dance, not only in the beauty of nature or the intimacy of a love relationship, but in every moment of every day of ordinary life. Spirituality can be found at the heart of the great religions and in no religion.

Personal Effort

Second, training for the spiritual life depends primarily on *personal effort*. The process of the first step on the path is to turn our soul from its egoistic state of consciousness absorbed in worldly attractions to a higher state in which the Divine can pour itself into our soul and transform it. The soul becomes "grace-filled." The potency of this step depends on the intensity of the turning, the power that directs our soul inward. The measures of that intensity are 1) the aspiration of our heart, 2) the determination of our will, and 3) the concentration of our mind.

Some people meditate at a certain time each day. This is a good idea, but actually we are our prayer every minute of the day. Everything we say or do, the way we open a door, the way we walk, the way we talk, are all our meditation and prayer. We need to become aware how often the spiritual life is or is not on our mind and in our heart.

At this step, Aurobindo suggests that we continue to read. Reading centers our thoughts and opens our mind to ways to proceed. If dogma is appealing, follow it. If dogma is not particularly appealing, we need to search and have the courage to experience. All experiences are steps on the path. When we feel as if we failed in something, we need to be attentive to our attitude. Kicking ourselves won't help, but making certain that we learned from our failure will help. Forgiving ourselves and forgiving others is of utmost importance. How do we learn to forgive? First, we must understand that whatever level of consciousness we are on, we all act in a way we think will benefit us. If a person is angry with us, yells at us, snubs us, swears at us, that person is acting out of ignorance. Our actions always show the degree of our spiritual development. Socrates said that it is better to be harmed by another than to harm another -- by harming another we damage our own soul.

Personal effort is the discipline of constantly remembering the divine. Ideally, we should identify with the Biblical phrase: "My zeal for the Lord has eaten me up." It is our zeal for the Lord, our heart's eagerness to attain the divine that consumes the ego. At this point we commence to view the world in a different way.

Establish Contact with God

The third step is to *establish contact with God*. When that happens, our personal effort gives way to awareness that is a force other than our own – a divine force or grace that transcends our ego is at work in us. Gradually we will learn to submit to this mysterious power. Finally we can say, "Thy will be done." Our own willful ego becomes one with the higher power – with God.

However, even when we think it is our own personal effort and aspiration at work in our lives, if we look more deeply, we realize it is always the divine at work. For instance, we may believe we are wise, courageous, virtuous, and discriminating. But that's our ego, which is only an instrument: wisdom, courage, virtue and the others really belong to our inner divine self. On the other hand, mistakes and failures are merely knots that we have tied in the divine's power. Aurobindo assures us that our identification with the ego is really ignorance and childishness. As we become more conscious, we will learn to trust the divine within (Christ, Buddha Nature, Atman). Such experience of the sacred does not hinge on a particular concept of God or religious observances: It depends on how we relate to ourselves and to each other -- on how we relate to the earth and the cosmos.

Spiritual Exercises

Spiritual exercises, such as meditation, prayer, yoga, and ho-

listic health all help transform our selfishness into selfless-
ness, our personal love into unconditional love, and our
opinions into knowledge. These exercises help us acknowledge both our humanity and our divinity, and they inspire a
reverence for life that enhances our capacity for love, peace,
and joy. Following the Eightfold Path, practicing the word
and personal effort all help us experience contact with God.
These spiritual exercises help us better understand lessons
the world classroom has to offer.

Jesus said, "Be in the world but not of it." The world is a
necessary and holy place for the soul to complete its human
pilgrimage, but we must be careful about desiring material
objects (cars, houses, clothes) at the expense of the spirit.
Material things are satisfying for the moment, but they cannot
fulfill our need for spiritual wisdom. We know that the world
can be an arduous testing ground and at the same time serve
as an inspiration for higher life. Aurobindo said the malady of
the world is that people cannot find their spiritual soul. We
know deep within that what he and all spiritual teachers say
is true. We look for happiness by pursuing wealth, recognition, and sensuous pleasure, when the only real happiness
lies in the truth, beauty, and goodness of God.

God's mystery is everywhere and nowhere. The world is
God's mystery. The world is holy and sacred. How can we be
separated from the boundless and inexpressible mystery?
Could what is boundless be apart from us? In H.P.Blavatsky's
words, the Divine "...thrills through every atom and infini-
tesimal point of the whole Cosmos." Thus God is both transcendent and immanent. When Jesus warned that we should
be in the world but not of it, wasn't he saying to partake in
the mystery and not get stuck in surface materialism? One
way to be in the world but not of it is to listen to our conscience. The Divine presence resides in each of us as the inner voice. Some teachers call it the "inner guide." This "still
small voice" is, unfortunately, easy to ignore.

We could liken the divinity in our soul to the bright sun.
In his dialogue, the *Allegory of the Cave,* Plato used the sun as
a symbol of Good (God), the source and author of all things.

The cave represents our state of ignorance. Borrowing that analogy, we could view each of us as a ray of the sun. However, separating us from the knowledge of the sun are many clouds: jealousy, anger, prejudice, ambition, lying, fear, laziness, selfishness, gossip, injustice, greed, and so on. Each cloud obstructs our ability to see the sun. We could call the clouds our cave of ignorance.

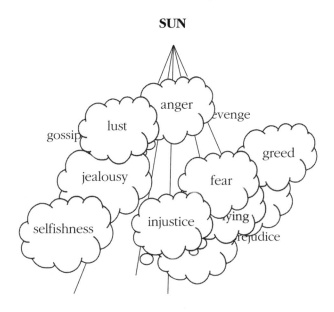

We think we are free and in control of our lives, yet we continually set up these obstacles that keep us from recognizing the divinity. And it is to this egoistic "freedom" that we become so attached. Our ego, boasting of freedom, is at every moment the ignorant slave, toy, and puppet of countless people, powers, and influences in the world. By letting go of the ego and surrendering our trust to that which transcends it, we would know and experience the Divine within. Florence Nightingale held that a belief in the universal law does not mean humankind is a helpless plaything of the divine, but that we are charged with discovering and exercising the laws by which the world is governed. We are fellow workers with the divine and directly responsible for our own fate – for creating our own destiny. Nightingale saw life as a self-correcting process, in which an omnipotent, omnipresent, and perfect God would, by means of universal law, ultimately lead humanity to perfection. Mistakes, she said, are naturally part of this self-correcting process. "Failure is essential on the road to success."

Complete freedom is the highest stage of spiritual life, and it isn't safe or in the least effective to begin with the highest stage. It is important to remember that at the beginning, the goal is only an idea and not a living truth in our lives. Yet, without an idea of the goal, our journey could not become a reality. Before we reach wholeness, we have to struggle with the darkness and distortions in our personal lives. If we deny the darkness (the shadow) we repress it and eventually it comes back to haunt us, especially in our projections on others. By recognizing the evil in ourselves and in the universe, but not getting caught up in it, we take a giant leap into awareness. Jung observed that, "Only by recognizing evil and its power can we refuse to succumb to its force." When Jesus said, "resist not evil," he was telling us not to get caught up in it. By resisting evil, by fighting against evil, we give it power.

We remake ourselves from the inside out. Jung wrote: "Only a blockhead concerns himself with the faults of another which can in no way be changed. The wise man looks inside of himself and asks: 'Who am I, that this should happen to me?'" When we study our own inner soul, rather than criticizing others, we begin to speak from the heart. We discover that when people speak from the heart, differences of personality, gender, race, class, education, religious and sexual preference fall away. We learn how our opinions limit us as well as define us.

Gradually the "me" drops out of our personal equation, and "you" takes its place. We aren't seeking happiness from others because we already have happiness within, and so what matters most to us is the other person's well-being. In the process we discover what inner obstacles hold us back from aspiring, loving, and giving fully, and we take action to remove those obstacles. Increasingly we give unconditionally from our hearts without holding back, putting on a persona, or expecting anything in return.

As we develop self-awareness and engage in serving others, we enter into an even broader spectrum of experience: we are part of the underlying order. We feel connected to something larger than ourselves, which seems to be moving and shaping our lives in ways we become increasingly aware of.

Spirituality presupposes certain qualities, including awareness of a transcendent dimension, a sense of wonder, love, and gratitude, as well as compassion and kindness. We do not have to deny our emotions, but we must learn to be responsible for them. We start trusting the wisdom of intuition. By disciplining our physical being, our desires, emotions, and thoughts into the right attitude, they will answer to the influences we choose.

Though the divinity is the source of everything, we need to train our egoistic energies to recognize their source. Then we can work at untying the knots that keep us thinking we are in total control of our lives and other lives as well. Through these spiritual exercises, our personal efforts will melt into the divine power at work in us.

The Divine Guide

Jesus spoke of the divine power as our inner guide. "The kingdom of God is within." "The father and I are one. As I am so can you be." "…you are gods." Depending upon the person, the inner guide may be experienced as an impersonal power or as a divine person. Our conception of God varies according to our needs and our state of consciousness.

As the turmoil of our egoistic life gives way to a calmer self-knowledge, we recognize more fully the divine light growing within us. We see how our entire life has been turning us toward the spiritual path. Even the obstacles and our struggles begin to make sense, as do our so-called successes and failure. We begin to appreciate those individuals who by hurting us jarred us into awareness and sensitivity. This is all part of the divinity molding us into God's own image.

At the beginning some of us can't see where we are being led and we revolt against the leading. Many years ago when I was in college, the profession that least interested me was teaching. But I got hooked on philosophy. After acquiring a master's degree and a Ph.D., I suddenly realized that unless I was independently wealthy, which I was not, I must acquire a job. The job available to me was teaching. I entered the classroom with fear and trepidation and the firm conviction that I would just hate teaching and would soon find a more stimulating career. I had not been in the classroom more than minutes when my fears crumbled. I loved it. Since then, I have been unspeakably grateful.

Fortunately, the divine guide isn't offended by our revolt or discouraged by our lack of faith or repelled by our weakness. Once we give our assent to the divinity, our lives become joy-filled. If we withdraw our assent, because it's difficult for us to believe in something unseen within ourselves, we cling to our ego and suffer the consequences. Of course it is easier for us to believe in something external and visible to the physical senses. That is why many people seek external support for their spiritual progress – some ritual or object of faith outside of themselves. Usually we call for a human intermediary as the divine manifestation in a human appearance, the incarnation of a Krishna, Christ, or Buddha, a prophet, teacher, or saint.

There is nothing wrong with these external aids, for they are necessary to awaken our soul to the divine within. However, it isn't sufficient to worship Krishna, Christ, or Buddha externally if we have not realized Krishna, Christ, or Buddha in ourselves. Spiritual teachers often say that one of the best ways to do inner work is to find our inner guide and get acquainted. They say: visualize your guide and he or she will gradually appear. Talk to your guide, and ask questions. Your guide is the living archetype of spirit within you. Your guide is your teacher. He or she will teach you your path to spirit if you ask. Your guide will not volunteer information. Socrates said his inner guide never told him what to do, but would always warn him if he was going in the wrong direction.

In Bernard Shaw's play, "*Saint Joan,*" the inquisitor, the Cardinal, says to Joan, "Forget your voices. Give this up... these voices are just your imagination." Joan looks up at him: "Yes, I know. That is the way God speaks to us."

Chapter Five

Journey of the Soul

One's greatest concern should be
to make the soul as good as possible.

Socrates

Angels and Dragons

*C*an another person ever tell us who we are or what we should become? Have you ever been told you are good or bad, smart or stupid, abnormal or an outsider? Was it ever proposed that you become an engineer, accountant, computer programmer, doctor, psychologist, nurse, or teacher? When others tell us what we should do with our lives, they are actually revealing part of themselves. If, through pressure, we accept what others say, we are cheating ourselves and in the long run cheating them. Until people reach very high spiritual realization, it is doubtful they know us as well as we know our self.

Knowing who we are takes a lot of strenuous soul-searching. Basically we are afraid – first of the hard work, and secondly of what we may find. The German philosopher Friedrich Nietzsche identified *fear* and *laziness* as the two culprits that hold us back from becoming our true selves. Nietzsche said most people are afraid to see that as human beings, we are both angel and devil, and as we delve deeply into our soul, we would necessarily experience shadows as well as light. Even if we are brave enough to admit our dual nature, it is easier to read about the problems of rich and famous people, drive-by shootings, and what is happening in the Near East than it is to probe deeply into our own psyche (soul).

According to Aurobindo, "No one can reach heaven who has not passed through hell." We can only reach as high up as we have reached low down. The higher we go, the lower we must plunge. If we don't look beneath the externals we continue to live unfulfilled lives. Saints have always written of the hellish temptations that accompany their breakthrough to spiritual bliss. The journey to self is so complex that often we do not know where to begin. We fear to meet inner dragons that might slay us before we slay them. Coming to terms with our dark side (the shadow) as we climb steep paths laden with obstacles seems almost overwhelming. We are so used to the security of the group – family, friends, church, and the work place – that the thought of an individual adventure of consciousness is frequently put on the back burner. In the words of Albert Einstein: "Few people are capable of expressing with equanimity opinions which differ from the prejudices of their social environment. Most people are even incapable of forming such opinions."

We know the world can be cruel, but it is also familiar and we prefer familiarity to the unknown. Parents may brutally condemn their children's actions or physically batter them, but more terrifying than the familiar brutality, is the unknown. I remember a young child so severely beaten by her mother that social workers came to remove the child to a foster home. As they were leaving with the child, the youngster frantically stretched both small bruised arms toward her mother and cried, "Mommy, Mommy, help me!" More terrifying than the familiar brutal beatings was the unknown. People tend to stay in destructive relationships for the same reason.

One of our strongest fears is what other people think of us. The world of condemnation may cause us suffering, but the spiritual world is unknown, therefore feared. The Danish existential philosopher Soren Kierkegaard aptly titled one of his books *Fear and Trembling*. If we decide to spend our energy searching out who we are, what would our friends and others think? On the other hand, if we allow the "crowd" to dictate to us, or allow fear to limit us, we miss a great deal on our adventure of consciousness. As Kierkegaard aptly stated, "The crowd is untruth."

OPEN MIND

Most of our search in the West has revolved around traditional Judeo-Christian thought. Other cultures and other belief systems were ignored or looked at with contempt. That
too is fear of the unknown. Events of the world are at our
fingertips, so why not ideas of the spiritual world? Hindu,
Buddhist, Taoist, and Native American belief systems have
existed for thousands of years. Greek philosophers such as
Socrates, Plato, and Aristotle, have survived the test of time.
Could they hold some truths for us?

To be part of this world is to understand it on a larger
scale. We would not want to discard all Christian beliefs because we may disagree with Catholicism on the infallibility of
the Pope. We would not claim that Protestantism has no re-
deeming value because fundamentalists believe gay life is the
product of the devil. No more would we reject Hindu thought
because some of them practice the caste system, or Islam for
its believers facing Mecca each day in prayer, or refuse to eat
health food because New Age spirituality touts it.

Taking the spiritual journey calls on us to be our own
person, to think things through for ourselves, to listen to the
quiet inner voice – even to know there is a quiet inner voice
– and to reject pabulum answers. We are called on to make
our own way, to use maps that will help guide us to our highest spiritual destination. The journey to know oneself – the
journey of the soul – is a pioneering adventure of consciousness.

Does the Soul Exist?

Interest in the soul can be traced all the way back to the beginning of humankind. People involved with the spiritual life
have always felt that the physical body is only part of what
makes up a human being. There is something that survives
the death of the physical body. Early shamans and seers believed that at death the soul leaves the physical body to abide
in another realm. They recognized the soul as the *life force*
that animated the body. As long as the life force was in the

body, the body lived. When the soul or life force left, then the body died. The soul, as the principle of life, could not die. This insight did not escape Helen Keller: "It gives me a deep comforting sense that things seen are temporal and things unseen are eternal."

Skeptics have always argued that the existence of the soul cannot be scientifically proved. But such a statement is a little like comparing apples and oranges. First, the soul is not a material object for scientists to study. Second, declared Aurobindo, the soul needs no scientific proof of its own existence. Those in the Newtonian era believed the soul was locked up in the body – in the head. French philosopher Rene Descartes thought that the seat of the soul is in the pineal gland. Today most behaviorists locate the soul in the cerebral cortex, about an inch away from the pineal gland. But is it scientifically, philosophically, or even theologically possible to locate the soul in the brain?

If we look to Genesis: "God breathed upon the waters," we realize that breath is life and life is psyche or soul. Thus soul is in everything and everywhere. Matthew Fox maintains, "The main problem in our culture now is that our work is too small for our souls, and our worship is too small for our souls, and our education is too small for our souls, and our politics and economics are too small for our souls. Except for that, we're in great shape."

In the thirteenth century, St. Thomas Aquinas wrote, "Every human mind is *capax universi"* – capable of the universe. The great mystic Meister Eckhart exclaimed, "God is delighted to watch your soul enlarge."

Plato's View of the Soul

The first person in the Western world to give a detailed explanation of the soul was Plato. His theory of the soul laid the foundation for all Western traditions. He wrote that the soul is our capacity for moral character and intelligence. Plato agreed with his teacher Socrates that our greatest concern should be to "make the soul as good as possible."

Plato's writings continue to have an immense influence on Christianity's belief that the soul consists of one unit made up of three parts. Plato said that all people experience confusion and conflict because there are three different kinds of activity going on in the soul. First is the rational part of the soul consisting of *reason* and *intuition.* This aspect of the soul gives us the ability to seek for knowledge of truth, beauty, and goodness. Next is the irrational aspect of the soul that contains two parts: the *spirited* (not *spiritual*) and the *appetites* (five senses – taste, touch, smell, hearing, sight). The spirited part is our drive toward action, which includes honor, glory, ambition, and recognition, and the appetite part of the soul, which consists of desires for things of the body as food, drink, shelter, and so on. The soul's unique function is to have each part in harmony with the other parts. For Plato, balance meant that the rational aspect of the soul controls the irrational aspects.

Plato was quick to notice that if the irrational soul takes charge, we experience various kinds of conflict. For instance, our desire to be what we want to be and our desire to be what others want us to be. Most of us would have little trouble finding ourselves caught in the tensions between emotions and mind, sensual and spiritual, individual and universal. The ultimate goal of the soul for Plato is knowledge of eternal truth, beauty and goodness. And this knowledge is the source – the very essence – of the soul itself. Because this knowledge lies within, we can't look outside ourselves in the external world to find it. Putting this inner knowledge into daily practice is the art of living.

In his dialogue *The Symposium,* Plato offered a humorous metaphor of human nature. There are three types of human beings: one wholly male, one entirely female, and a third type made up of both male and female. They each had four hands and feet and formed a circle, one head with two faces. The gods, fearful of human power, cut them in two. Each half went about pursuing its other half searching for wholeness. The female soul searches for its other half in a female, the male soul searches for a male, and the male/female soul searches for its opposite. The story implies that originally human nature was one and whole and if we are to find happiness and wholeness again in the world, we must obey God -- the source of truth, beauty and goodness. Being split in two, i.e., exiled from God, is the underlying theme of human nature in Western traditions. Jewish philosopher Martin Buber stressed the idea of individuality when he said, "Everyone must come out of his Exile in his own way."

Finally, Plato wrote that the kind of life we choose depends upon what the soul loves. Sincere spiritual love brings joy whereas selfish personal love brings conflict. Selfish love results when the irrational portion of the soul, made up of emotions and physical desires, takes control of our lives. Being neutral, the will or spirited part of the soul responds to the stronger pull. It either follows the lead of our sensuous desires and selfishness, or it soars in the wake of reason and intuition toward the true beauty of universal love.

Hindu View of the Soul

The *Upanishads*, a Hindu scripture asks, "What am I in my deepest existence? I may appear to be a physical body, but is that what I really am? Is the 'I' that thinks the self to be a physical body also physical? Isn't the 'I' more properly the self (soul) than the body?" The philosophers of the *Upanishads* explained there is no such thing as an individual "I." What we think as "I" is the ego. Although the ego seems real now, it is actually transitory or changing all the time.

An engaging story in the *Chandogya Upanishad* illustrates the concept that the soul is something more than meets the eye:

> A boy asked his father how a self [soul] that could not be seen could possibly be our true nature. In order to teach his son, the father gave him a lump of salt to drop into a cup of water. The boy did as his father asked. Later the father asked his son to pick the lump of

salt out of the water and give it back to him. When the boy could not find it, he said the salt was not there.

The father then requested his son to drink some of the water. The boy swallowed the salty water from the cup and realized that the salt, although it could not be seen, was indeed in every part of the water – just as the self [soul] is present in us and in the universe.

Hindu philosophers describe the soul as higher and lower: the higher or Divine Soul (Atman) is our true self in unity with Brahman (God). The lower aspects of the soul consist of the three modes in nature: *sattwic* (reason), *rajas* (desire), and *tamas* (inertia). For the Hindus, the Divine is our true "I" that contains unconditional love and spiritual wisdom. The closer the worldly part of our soul comes to knowing these qualities, the greater is our capacity for the spiritual life. "The spirit down here in man and the spirit up there in the sun, in reality are only one spirit, and there is no other one," say the *Upanishads*.

Buddhist View of the Soul

With the exception of Buddhism, which suggests we have no permanent individual soul, Eastern and Western ideas of what the soul is, the reason for its existence, and the way it functions, are strikingly similar. Buddhism holds that the human being is a collection of five *skandhas*: body, feelings, perceptions, dispositions, and consciousness. Material elements make up the physical body. Feelings include sensations, both pleasant and unpleasant. Perceptions are sense perceptions – sight, hearing, touch, taste, and smell. Dispositions are mental activities present in consciousness – fear, hatred, and love. Higher states of consciousness occur in the realm of thoughts, ideas, and virtue. What we call the soul is actually a combination of these skandhas. There is no personal salvation as such. There is, upon enlightenment, the experience of *nir-*

vana (bliss). Reaching nirvana is the goal of the Buddha's teachings.

Chinese View of the Soul

Lao Tzu, the founder of Taoism, placed emphasis on the mystical aspect of nature. The Taoists look to Tao (God) that is in nature and in them for wisdom. Since Tao is the source of the natural flow of nature and the source of our true selves or souls, the key to self-identity, and therefore happiness, is to "go with the flow." The way of the Tao is called "the simple way."

Confucius, the Chinese humanist philosopher, believed that the goal of all human beings is to be happy and to live the good life, and that *Jen* and *Li*, the two basic principles needed to live the good life are found within all people. Jen is the source of all human actions, and Li is the principle of order in social life and morality. The conscious combination of Jen and Li is true self-identity.

Jewish View of the Soul

Judaism emphasizes the unity of mind and body, eschewing a body-soul duality. Unlike Descartes, who had great difficulty reconciling the opposition of mind and body within human beings, Jews believe that the mind and body are a unit and not divided into a thinking substance and a physical substance. In response to the age-old question, "Which shall people gratify, their flesh or the soul?" Judaism answers, "Both."

In the beginning God created human beings from the dust of the earth, then breathed into them a living spirit (soul). Rather than observing the soul as salt dissolved in the divine waters, as the Hindus, the Jews cast themselves into a partnership with their God through a divine covenant. God gave human beings free will to choose to be wicked or virtuous. The true soul is found in the good will.

Christian View of the Soul

In Christianity, human beings have a dual nature – angel and devil. Pascal called the human person "a monster, a chimera, the glory and the shame of the universe." This paradoxical vision is based on the story of human creation and the fall in Genesis. Humanity is the glory of God's work. "God created man in his own image, in the image of God he created him; male and female he created them" (Gen. 1:27). Human beings are *like* God, but they are *not* God. Adam and Eve perverted that *likeness* by disobeying their creator. Therefore, except for some Christian mystics who identify soul with God, the human soul is other than God.

In his famous book, *The City of God*, St. Augustine maintained that before the fall of Adam, humans possessed both the ability not to sin and the ability to sin. Since the fall, all humans are sinners and we can do nothing to save ourselves from this bondage to sin. Only God's freely given grace can redeem the soul from its sin.

For the Christian mystic point of view we turn to St. Francis of Assisi: "What we are looking for is what is looking."

Islamic View of the Soul

According to Islam, Allah (God) makes human beings from a blood clot or a drop of sperm (*Koran:* Sura 96). This clot of blood or sperm contains the necessary ingredients for living in the world and submitting to the will of Allah. Islam perceives three aspects in human nature: 1) The animal soul that is the source of desire and belongs to the lower part of the personality – to the flesh, 2) The spirit or vital life that animates the human body, and 3) Reason, the spiritual faculty of the soul used to discern right and wrong. Sufi mystics include the heart faculty by which one unites the true soul with Allah through love.

Unlike Christians, Muslims do not believe that the human soul is alienated from Allah as a result of the fall and people do not carry the burden of original sin. In order to realize the true self or essence of one's soul, it is up to each individual to remember Allah in every aspect of daily life, and to fulfill His will. Muslims who carry Allah in their hearts more readily open to the spiritual soul that is a channel between the Lord and the world.

Eastern and Western Differences

Between the Eastern and Western traditions there is a subtle but immense difference. The Christian would never say, "I am Christ," but will confess with Paul, "Not I, but Christ lives in me." Here, there is no destruction of the ego, but a possession by God. The ego becomes a servant of God. The Eastern spiritual experience requires complete removal of the individual ego. The Buddhist sutra says, "Thou wilt know that thou art the Buddha." The Hindu Upanishad teaching says, "I am Brahman (God)."

As Westerners, Jung thought that we need the ego to know the transcendent unity of the self. And to reach enlightenment the ego needs to subordinate itself to the Transcendent Self (Divine Soul). In the West, this is the basis for mystical experience. It is similar to the Chinese Taoists. In Taoism, individuals who reach the divine soul or self transpose the ego by penetrating the "magic circle" of dualities (yin/yang), then return to the undivided Tao. This is similar to Plato's explanation of the perfect being – round on all sides and uniting within oneself the two sexes. In the Jewish, Christian, and Islam traditions, Adam and Eve are archetypal (prototypes of humanity) human beings who must fall from their unconscious state of bliss into conscious existence.

THE QUEST

Sages from many religious and philosophical traditions agree that we humans have the opportunity to grow or evolve to greater consciousness and spiritual living. They believe that we humans are here on earth to experience matter, life, and mind in space/time. In his book *Spectrum of Consciousness,* Ken Wilber writes: "A full spectrum approach to human consciousness and behavior means that men and women have available to them a spectrum of knowing – a spectrum that includes, at the very least, the eye of flesh, the eye of mind, and the eye of spirit."

Through the world medium we acquire what we need to grow spiritually and to raise everything on earth to a higher spiritual level. We have the ability to elevate the consciousness of other people, domestic pets, wild animals, plants, and if the Native Americans are correct, even rocks. We affect the consciousness of the whole earth. The more conscious consideration we show to ourselves, the easier it is to show kindness to others. As we know a lack of consideration, like a few sour notes, can ruin a beautiful piece of music.

I particularly like the analogy that the world is a symphonic orchestra and each one of us is an instrument in the orchestra. Some of us are violins, others saxophones, trumpets, cellos, drums, pianos, bassoons, until every imaginable instrument is included. I envision each instrument as learning how to play Beethoven's Ninth. Some instruments make mistakes -- others rebel against the conductor's score and complain that the cellos should sound more like the violins. The clarinets insist they have better tone quality than the piccolos, and the pianos threaten to strike if harps are given equal time.

In my imagination, some of the orchestra members are learning to read the music and others insist on playing by ear. There are beginners, intermediates, and advanced -- all playing Beethoven's Ninth symphony at the same time. How does the music sound? We hear a few pure notes, but most of the instruments are off key. They still have a lot to learn. Does the same condition apply to the world of human souls at this stage in our evolution? When each instrument (soul) finally masters the score and becomes one with the essence of music, the world symphonic orchestra will play in glorious harmony. That's our goal.

Internal Conflict

Until the soul is working in total harmony, we continue to

experience internal confusion and conflict. Some of our conflicts are moral. Is it ever right to lie, to gossip, to cheat a competitor, or use another person to our own advantage? Moral awareness about right and wrong can be agonizing, but once we are aware of these internal conflicts we are on the road to making true conscious choices.

Our conflicts do not have to be moral ones. Imagine that you desire just one more dessert. Your reason says, "Remember, you are trying to lose weight, one more dessert won't help." Whether you choose to indulge your taste or choose rationally to not eat an extra dessert depends upon your will to give in to the senses or listen to reason. It takes a strongly disciplined mind to say "no" and mean "no" to sense desires. Anyone who has tried to stop smoking knows how much power the senses have. It takes a while, but after long bouts of discipline, the mind even begins to enjoy making rational choices and as a result it will eventually subdue the senses.

A Change in Consciousness

Aurobindo perceived the soul as a spark of the divinity that supports our growth out of ignorance into light. By ignorance he meant that we have yet to attain all knowledge, love and wisdom. Light is a metaphor for truth, beauty, and goodness. As with Plato, the instruments of the soul are the mind, emotions, and body. The soul itself is immortal and passes from life to life (see Ch. 7) carrying the essence of our experience. Most of us know how to reason, but for Aurobindo it is important at this point in our evolution to develop an even higher faculty – *intuition*. Intuition helps us through agonizing over right and wrong. An intuition is a direct knowing that skips the step-by-step reasoning process.

Saints and sages have always said that intuition is a higher faculty than reason. Through intuition comes revelation. With intuition we may not know exactly how we know, but we know. It is a little like magic. The intuitive faculty envisions the completed puzzle, not just a piece of the puzzle here and there. However, we frequently don't trust hunches and quickly brush them aside. Again, this is our fear of the unknown. Einstein intuited the theory of relativity, but it took him fifteen years to work the theory out in a formula applied to reason for mathematicians and physicists. The intuition itself probably lasted only a minute or less, but in that flash, Einstein perceived the relativity of the universe.

The reason aspect of the soul follows the laws of logic. With reason we structure language, build computers, and organize corporations. Scientific researchers use reason to advance technology and medicine; philosophers analyze theories and moral constructs, and politicians decide government policy. Most of us use reason to figure out the grocery list and decide whether we can afford to buy a new car.

Recall that for Plato, the five senses comprise the lower portion of the irrational aspect of the soul. The five senses are close to the physical world, thus relate only to the physical world. Our sensuous nature is so powerful that many people identify themselves with the physical body. When a body can no longer breathe, we pronounce the person dead. We say, "Poor Jud is dead," not "Jud's body is dead." Seldom do we say, "Jud has left his body," or "Jud has made the transition called death." In the absence of a loved one's physical body, we experience loneliness. That is how closely we relate to the physical being. Even if a body is kept alive by machines and other vital signs are absent, we think of the person as alive. Is it any wonder that the spiritual life is so obscure when we separate spirit from matter by believing that humans and animals and nature are physical only?

If we shift our perspective of thinking that the soul is in the body, we could realize with Aurobindo, Plato, St. Thomas Aquinas, Hildegard of Bingen, and Meister Eckhart, among others, that *the soul is not in the body, the body is in the soul – the universal soul.*

For Plato the irrational part of the soul is the root of our emotions and willpower. Because it is neutral, the spirited can follow either our selfish ego desires or follow our spiritual aspirations, whichever is stronger. Our ego desires are mainly personal. If you want to be a millionaire by the age of forty, your personal willpower waxes strong and employs the reason part of your soul to structure the best course for making a million dollars. In this case both the reason and the spirited parts of the soul will serve the appetites. It takes courage to produce the willpower necessary for spiritual growth.

German philosopher Immanuel Kant wrote that our moral worth is rooted in *goodwill.* An example of goodwill is never using other persons for our own selfish benefit, but always seeing others as "ends-in-themselves." Kant is reiterating what Confucius and Jesus taught long ago: *Do unto others as you would have them do unto you.*

THE SOUL AND LOVE

Most philosophers and sages believe that the core of the soul is *love.* Plato suggested that each portion of the soul expresses love in its own way through the physical senses, the spirited, and the rational. Before the soul as a whole unit can experience divine love, it must move from the constricted ties of physical love to the freedom of unconditional love.

Love is the energy force of the soul, said Teilhard de Chardin. Hate is merely love gone astray. For example, some people in our society believe that homosexuality ought to be condemned. By seeking to dominate gays with their morals, they project their own anger and fear. Recall that we project what we cannot accept in ourselves. Many men are afraid to love other men, except as business associates or fellow teammates. But true love does not have to be only sexual or even sexual at all. True love is spiritual. Each part of the soul expresses love in its own way. The sensuous part of the soul loves the external physical body and things of the physical world. The spirited aspect of the soul loves a friend's character. The highest part of the soul loves truth, beauty, and goodness, thus sees it within everything and everyone.

Saint Paul may have said it best: "Love is patient; love is kind... love is never rude... it is not prone to anger... Love does not rejoice in what is wrong but rejoices with the truth."

Love is the inner journey of the soul

Chapter Six

What Goes Around
Comes Around
(Karma)

Be not deceived; God is not mocked:
for whatever a man soweth,
that shall he also reap.

Galatians 6.7

Justice

*H*ave you ever asked yourself if there is any justice in the world? How is it that the wicked prosper and the virtuous suffer? Why is an innocent baby born with a malformed body? What brings misfortune and pain to a good person? In Judeo-Christian terms, if God is all-good, all-knowing, and all-powerful, why does God permit evil and unmerited suffering to exist?

No matter how we rationalize why evil happens to good people, it makes no sense unless we look at God and the world in a new way. In the Far East, the universal law of justice is called karma. In the Western world, karma is known as the law of "cause and effect," or "action and reaction." Theosophists consider karma the twin doctrine to reincarnation.

Students of reincarnation maintain that the appearance of injustice in the world is the result of our limited knowledge and vision. If rather than one lifetime only, we could see the whole series of an individual's reincarnations and the workings of that person's karma from life to life we would see that justice indeed rules the world. There is no such thing as chaos, luck, or random chance.

What is Karma?

What exactly is karma? Today we often hear the word karma bandied about: "good karma," "bad karma," "quick karma." While karma has found a place in our contemporary vocabulary what one means by it is not always consistent. In its popularized version, karma may suggest luck, fate, or destiny. The bottom line, however, is very simple whether we go back two thousand years to "What you sow you also reap," or walk college campuses today and hear, "What goes around comes around." That's karma!

Philosophers of reincarnation and karma believe three kinds of karmic laws affect us: 1) those operating in our present life, 2) those held over from past lives, and 3) those stored up for future lives. The life into which we are born depends on the choices we made in a previous life, or previous lives, and at every moment in this life we are shaping our characters and destinies for future lives. Thus, we carry with us the whole of our past as we now create our future.

Originally karma was an ancient word meaning the *law of action and reaction.* Over the centuries people have called karma many things. Scientists refer to it as the *law of cause and effect.* Philosophers write about the *universal law of justice.* Theologians look to Scripture, *"...the measure with which you measure will be used to measure you"* (Matt. 7:2). Taoists use a practical phrase, *the natural law of balance,* and Buddhists explain karma as *the wheel of the law.*

Thus karma signifies universal order. When Einstein said, "God doesn't play dice," he implied that the universe is a mathematically ordered system. That is why we can send astronauts into space and why we can measure the distance between planets. The law of karma is the divine law that says our universe is at peace when there is equilibrium. When a person does something to disturb this equilibrium, a reaction takes place.

Realms of Karma

Disorder may occur in the physical realm, the emotional

realm, the mental realm, and the moral realm. Just as cause and effect is the law of the physical world, so the law of karma governs the results that follow upon the choices we make in all realms of our being. For example, *just* or *kind* actions bring reconciliation, while *unjust* or *unkind* actions produce alienation. According to the law of karma, there are no short cuts to becoming a complete and whole human being. If there are no short cuts, then we are exactly where we should be in this life. At this very moment we are reaping the results of our past karma on the physical, emotional, mental, and moral planes. And, by our present attitude we are creating future karma. Taoist sages found that our own thoughts and actions make our heaven and hell.

The law of karma is as impersonal as the law of gravity. If you jump off a cliff, the gravitational force pulls you down. The law of gravity doesn't question why you jumped – it merely draws you down. The same is true of the law of karma. If I commit a moral wrong, I am out of balance and must pay the debt. Karma does not question why I chose to be immoral. Because it is a universal law, a divine law, God's law, there is no ducking karma – or if you prefer, what we sow we also reap. The law operates in all human realms. If I have an evil thought, that imbalance could affect my emotions, mind, morals, and body. As the Buddha said, "All that we are is the result of what we have thought."

Imagine a woman named Jennifer Long. Jennifer is a conscientious citizen and volunteers her time at Memorial Hospital. She is popular with the staff and the patients. However at home, Jennifer lies to her spouse about her relationship with another man. In this life or in her next life, she will reap the results of her actions. Someone may cheat on Jennifer, or she may work hard to make a relationship work and her efforts fail. She may blame her companion or other persons, but if Jennifer understands the law of karma, she will realize that she has brought this "soured relationship" on herself. Of course that doesn't mean all of Jennifer's life would fail. She is popular and helps people feel better. She has lots of friends. Jennifer could be reaping karma on both counts.

Believers in karma tend to label their fortunes and misfortunes as "good karma" or "bad karma." But karma is neither good nor bad, it is an opportunity to balance our lives – a learning experience. Once we learn a lesson, we no longer need to experience karma in that area.

Mental Karma

Our thoughts do not go unheeded. We may never mention what we are thinking, but a thought is a powerful soul impression. You may secretly desire to have an affair with someone you meet at a party, and even if you say nothing about your lusty thoughts to anyone, you have tipped the scales of balance – of justice. As Jesus warned, we don't have to indulge in the act to commit adultery, because even secretly thinking about it separates us from our divine nature.

Based on Jesus' words, some religious Fundamentalists view AIDS as God's revenge on gay men. Does God take revenge? Not according to the law of karma. Our own choices tip the scales of balance. Unfortunately we are not fully conscious of the Christ within us, so our choices are often selfish or geared to personal pleasures. Catholic philosopher Teilhard de Chardin suggested that the creation is not yet finished, i.e., the creation is still going on. According to Teilhard de Chardin human beings are at the ego-mind stage evolving toward the more spiritual Christ consciousness. We could say that we are like teenagers growing into adulthood. As mere teenagers in this vast universe we try numerous experiments to reach divine love.

When we feel wounded by our parents or society and the wound is raw with anger or rage, we must deal with it. We ought not sweep it under the rug or the rage and anger could continue to deform our soul. If coming to terms with the source of our anger means asking for forgiveness or offering it, then that is what we must do. We must go through the pain that is necessary – go through the burning to get into the loving place in our soul where we are whole and not wounded. Then we can realistically deal with the issues that we allowed to limit our lives. We need to accept ourselves before we can love anyone else.

No matter what the problem, it is of no use to moan, "Why me? I don't deserve this." According to "whatever you sow you also reap," we do deserve it – whatever it is. As we gain this insight into life's mystery, we begin to realize that all events and relationships serve as catalysts. They move us beyond the limitations of ordinary "poor me" perception to a higher level of awareness. Wounding may be a spiritual message telling us it is time to move out of our ordinary way of viewing the world into a higher state of consciousness.

THE LENSES WE WEAR

According to German philosopher Immanuel Kant, *perception* is our own set of lenses through which we see the world. Since no two sets of lenses are the same prescription, we never know exactly how another person perceives the world. We habitually think that everyone sees things alike, but Kant proved that we each experience world events and objects in the world differently. As a result, we think about what we experience in our own personal way and are surprised when others respond differently.

For safety, we join groups that seem to interpret the world as we do. However, within the group no two members perceive anything exactly alike. If you are a Republican you agree with your group on fundamental government policies. If you are a Democrat you agree with other Democrats on the importance of human rights. But how far human rights should go depends on how liberal, moderate, or conservative individual members are. Splits within the party occur because people do not perceive the world in the same way. Even among the factions, no two liberals view policy exactly alike, nor do two conservatives. One conservative may consider stem cell research an important advance for curing diseases, another conservative agrees, but with strict limitations.

Notice how people view God. The socialist philosopher Karl Marx and psychiatrist Sigmund Freud wrote that human beings create God in their own image as a crutch. When humankind matures, they said, people won't need a God. Carl G. Jung, on the other hand, saw God as an archetype in the soul that people strive to discover. Joseph Smith believed God is a personal being made of flesh and bones. Moses described God as Spirit. Fundamentalists think of God as totally Other – separated from humankind and the world. Mystics experience God's presence in the world and in everything. Buddhists do not believe in a personal anthropomorphic god, but in a spiritual principle that pervades the universe. For the Taoist, the Tao is Non-being and Being, an impersonal principle of balance. And among all of the above are varieties upon the theme. That is why we have hundreds of Christian Protestant denominations, each differing in its perception of God, the world, and humankind.

Recall Kant and the various ways we view objects in the phenomenal world. How many times have you called a color red and your friend called the same color orange or rose? And we have differences of opinion about temperature: On a crisp autumn day, individuals unaffected by the weather wear short sleeve shirts. Those more sensitive to chill air slip on a jacket. Personal tastes differ radically. I like avocados and artichokes. One friend detests both and another likes artichokes, but breaks out in a rash from avocados. Our individual likes and dislikes are based on the accumulation of experiences brought from the past into the present.

Not long ago I watched a television talk show about career mothers versus mothers who choose to stay home full-time with their children. For an hour the mothers argued, defending their positions and criticizing the opposition. At the end of the program no mother had changed her mind, and none of the mothers had taken into consideration the unique individuality of her children. It seems to me that each child has different expectations, but none of these women saw the world as I do. Kant may have a good point concerning the lenses we wear. And thank goodness for our individual perceptions. Think of it. If everyone perceived the world identically, there would be unanimous agreement on what constitutes the true religion, the proper education, and contemporary lifestyle. We would have identical IQ's, creative ability, and personal interests. Imagine a world of think-a-likes – of human robots. As dull and joyless as it sounds, some people continue to condemn others for not thinking and acting the same as they do. Many groups believe: *there is our way and the wrong way.* But such limited perception takes away individual responsibility by insisting that all group members agree on what is best for everyone else.

Isn't there greater freedom when we take responsibility for the way we think and allow others to think the way they do without passing negative judgments on them? When two or more people stand in opposition, a synthesis can be found when all members listen and try to understand. On a larger scale, world harmony will be most wholesome when we share diversified ideas and integrate them into a unified network, as we do today with the Internet via computers. Though we experience life in our own unique way, by listening to and observing others, we could better understand why they act as they do. Jesus said, "If you want to avoid judgment, stop passing judgment. Your verdict on others will be the verdict passed on you..." (Matt. 7: 1-2)

Actions and Results

Scientists rely on the law of cause and effect to help them probe into the structure of the physical world. Physics demonstrates that no particle of energy can be put forth anywhere without a result following. A stone tossed in the air returns to earth. Winding an old-fashioned clock will produce a delayed result with exactly the same amount of force as the original energy expended. In mixing chemicals, the reaction may be immediate or delayed, but the reaction *will* occur.

Karma operates when we are conscious of it and when we are unconscious of it. By the functioning of karma, we shape our destiny. In the 1920's big business boomed, and to increase profits industries carelessly polluted the environment with chemical waste. The trend continued, and today these same industries must use a percentage of their profits to clean up the mess. Exploiting nature means exploiting ourselves:

what goes around comes around. Daily we weave the threads of our own and the earth's destiny. As Chief Seattle said: "Man did not weave the web of life, he is merely a strand in it. Whatever he does to the web, he does to himself."

Aurobindo emphasized that the law of karma teaches, it does not punish, and we are learning that breathing poisoned air and endangering wildlife is a threat to the earth's survival. If we want to walk barefoot on a beach or enjoy a romantic picnic, we must pick up the litter. Mining companies have learned to respect the land by replanting trees and shrubs after strip-mining because flora and fauna create a healthy environment. Our neglect and destruction constantly remind us to take action to protect the natural beauty and resources of mother earth.

Attitude

Emotions also are part of karma. Strong emotions include ambition, competition, recognition, success, acceptance, and possession. The quality of our emotional desires depends on the individual. I may desire to serve my country, but do I desire to serve because others will look up to me as a patriot, or do I serve out of duty to preserve a free land? I may desire to serve the poor and needy, the starving and sick, but do I serve them for personal recognition, or do I serve unselfishly? Desire motives are difficult to distinguish. I may believe my motives are pure, but if I search deeper, I could find a self-serving ego. Whatever my motives, karma will return the results of my *real* desires whether I am conscious or unconscious of them. In the *Bhagavad-Gita*, Lord Krishna reminds us not to look to the consequences of our actions. Motive alone is the key.

Both the Buddha and Jesus emphasized forging beyond our ego-oriented personality into the spiritual life. If we ignore the spiritual life by clinging to our ego personality, we continue to upset the universal harmony and must reap the results. If I resent a person even slightly, I am out of balance. And, if I deny the resentment I feel, I'm out of balance. If I allow a person's words to injure me, my ego is in control.

Jesus admonished us to *turn the other cheek*. A hard saying. He realized fully how difficult and rare it is to maintain a balance.

Accepting others with all their faults is no easy task. Usually we try to turn them around to see things our way, but it doesn't take long to recognize how futile that is. Perhaps the best way to accept others is by accepting ourselves. The way we perceive ourselves is the way we view others. If I don't trust myself, how can I trust someone else? If I am hard on myself, I judge others harshly. Why do we lash out at automobile drivers that cut us off? We find plenty of excuses, but have you ever cut someone off, either in a car or in a conversation? We tend to lash out at others when we do not accept ourselves. Thus our attitude tells us in no uncertain terms what we are.

A college student once told me whenever he went to a Circle K convenience market he ended up in a fight. He blamed it on the type of guys that hang out at Circle K. Do you get into fights when you frequent a convenience market? Did he attract the fights to himself? We take our attitude with us wherever we go.

There is a wonderful attitude story of a Chinese farmer who had an old horse he used to plow his fields:

> One day the horse of a Chinese farmer escaped into the hills. His neighbors sympathized with him for his bad luck. The farmer shook his head: "Good luck, bad luck. Who knows?"
>
> Later, the plow horse returned with a herd of wild horses from the hills. His neighbors congratulated the farmer on his good luck. The farmer shook his head: "Good luck, bad luck. Who knows?"
>
> When the farmer's son tried to tame one of the wild horses, the horse kicked him and broke his leg. The farmer's neighbors thought this was bad luck indeed. But the farmer said,

"Bad luck or good luck, who knows?"

A few weeks later the army marched into the village to induct every able-bodied youth. When they rejected the farmer's son because of his broken leg, the neighbors congratulated him on his good luck. Again the farmer shrugged his shoulders. "Good luck, bad luck. Who knows?"

Accepting things as they are opens us to possibilities we otherwise would not have if we judge people and events as good or bad. Karmic effects may not be felt immediately. Like a seed that lies dormant, the effect may sprout either in this life or in a future life. Presently we must deal with the seeds we have sown in the past, and our attitude toward life's ups and downs will sow the seeds of our future. Great hope lies in the law of karma. We may travel along as fast or as slow as we choose. A sincere change in attitude, a sincere act of forgiveness, can lighten our karmic load in the twinkle of an eye. Our greatest obstacle is the fear of letting go. We are so used to guilt, anxiety, depression, and special neuroses that we are afraid to set them aside and walk off without them.

THE WORLD IS A STAGE

In this stage of our evolution most of us are not aware of why we are in the circumstances we are in. However, philosophers and sages from all cultures have offered us guidance we could use for spiritual growth. Stoic philosophers thought the most important goal in life was to discover the role we are here on earth to play. "All the world is a stage and we are actors on the stage," said Stoic philosopher Epictetus (and later Shakespeare). A bit part should be played as perfectly as a major part because all parts are needed to complete the world tapestry. The tiny center of a flower may be invisible to the naked eye, but the hummingbird is attracted to its sweet nectar.

Whether the world recognizes us is unimportant. The

Stoics taught us not to worry about things we cannot change, such as the color of our eyes, date of birth, old age, death, or even the events that immediately face us. The greatest freedom we have is the ability to control our attitude. We can be courageous or cowardly in the role of life. Our attitude makes all the difference in whether we would be happy or miserable. For more than two thousand years the teachers of wisdom have said that daily we shape our karma – we reap what we sow. Heeding their words may be difficult, but it seems to make sense.

Chapter Seven

Reincarnation

All the world's a stage,
and all the men and women merely players.
They have their exits and their entrances
and one man in his time plays many parts,
his acts being seven ages.

William Shakespeare

Reincarnation: Fact or Fiction?

*T*he idea of reincarnation or rebirth is almost as old as human thought, and its origin is unknown. Whether we accept the theory as soul experience or reject it as hoop- la, the doctrine of reincarnation will likely endure as long as human beings continue to think about the meaning of life. However, there have been some grotesque interpretations of reincarnation. Some people used to believe, and some continue to believe that rebirth means at death the human soul transmigrates into a bird, a guinea pig, an ass, or a cockroach. The ancient Greeks called rebirth *metempsychosis*, which means the individual soul is born again, but always into a new human body, never into a less conscious creature. What good would it do for the human soul to return to the body of an animal or insect that has no reasoning ability? If the soul goes into an animal that has no ability to reflect upon its thoughts and actions, what important moral lessons could it learn? Rebirth philosophers argue that evolution always spirals upward – once a human always a human. We may have to work on an inferior aspect of our development in a lifetime, but we never lose our human capacities.

Reincarnation may explain déjà vu. Have you had the experience of remembering a place you have never been before? You could be driving along then suddenly be overpowered by the sensation that you have been in just that place before or that around the next curve you will recognize the exact house and scenery. Or have you ever been introduced to a person that seemed like an old friend? It is an amazing experience. Though psychologists offer a variety of explanations for déjà vu, reincarnation is a possible one.

Predispositions

If it is the purpose of each soul to become whole or perfect, how is it possible to gain this level of consciousness in one short lifetime? According to Aurobindo, if we are born only once, we face living in the present without any ties to the past except through physical heredity and written history. But could one life explain our innate tendencies? Most of us have irrational likes and dislikes, and sometimes we react with spontaneous fear. Something quite ordinary like crossing bridges or standing at the edge of a cliff may evoke a sense of panic in us. In some people, heights and fire and certain animals evoke unexplained fear. There seems to be no logical explanation for such reactions. They just happen.

On a larger scale we find historic *predispositions*. The people of America are often compared to the citizens of ancient Rome. We, as they, built an empire from small provincial beginnings. We have diverse cultures and strong military strength and commerce. America excels in building roads and structures similar to the Romans. Our period often reflects Roman culture, especially our virtues and vices. If students of reincarnation and karma are correct and nothing happens by chance, then many of us have been reborn in the same time and place as those with whom we formed past-life ties in Rome or other cultures in other lives.

Is it possible to trace our innate dispositions to biological heredity? Heredity is the transference of physical form and biological characteristics from one entity to another: as the flower so the seed, as the seed so the flower. A horse generates a horse, never a zebra or rhinoceros. A human generates a human, not an orangutan or beetle. Thus, physical transference of family and individual characteristics is easily observed. But as soon as a child begins to develop, a new and independent factor comes in, which is not its parents nor its ancestry, nor past humanity, but its own self. What matters most in life may not be our heredity, but what we make of our heredity. The past humanity is in us, but we ourselves are the artists of our lives. Our present environment certainly influences us: we are programmed, changed, and partly recreated by it. However, what counts in our soul journey is what we make of the environment and not what it makes of us. Students of reincarnation would say that we are drawn by our past thoughts and actions into these present individual and historical conditions. Our heredity, environment, and predispositions such as likes and dislikes, talents, intelligence, fears, and obstacles are a result of the choices we have made. We are born into the family, race, nation, and gender that best suits our soul's growth through evolution. Reincarnation could be the history of humankind, of each individual in the universe, and the part we play in our history is self-created.

If each soul is on a journey to wholeness, then parents do not give their child its soul. The child is a soul already. Parents furnish their child with the genes for a new body and the environment best suited for its individual needs. Based on past life attitudes, each person brings to their present life unique soul qualities, such as character, abilities, and needs. Reincarnationists suggest that the soul will come to a family with similar characteristics that give it the opportunity for further growth. Since parents and children are connected by past actions, the child would inherit biological tendencies, but the child's character would be significantly different. The children in a particular family may look alike physically, but each child has his or her own particular character, intellectual capacity, interests, and creative ability. No two children are alike. No two people are alike. Could even two clones be identical? They might share the same biological functions, but could they possibly share the same soul?

We all know that two children of the same parents who are raised in the same household turn out to be quite different in their likes and dislikes. One child is a natural tennis player, the other loves Egyptian art. One child excels in mathematics and almost flunks English while the other child considers English easy and mathematics perplexing. One child is extremely shy, the other child very outgoing. Even identical twins often have different interests and talents.

One of the explanations of genius and creative ability appearing in families lacking these qualities is reincarnation. Artist Salvador Dali remembered a past life when he was St. John of the Cross. Napoleon said he had been Charlemagne. General Patton had experienced certain battlefield areas before and knew that he had lived as a military officer in a past life. Blind Tom, a child born into poverty, had great musical ability that his parents did not have. Bach was a genius born into a family with no known past geniuses. Haydn played and composed at six years of age, and Mendelssohn at nine. Coleridge was reading the Bible at three, and John Stuart Mill began the study of Greek at three and read Xenophon, Herodotus, and Plato by the time he was eight years old. Tennyson and Goethe were writing poetry when they were eight, and Lope de Vega dictated verses at the age of five before he could write. Sonja Henie was the figure-skating champion of Norway when she was ten years old and world champion at fifteen. Norbert Wiener entered college at eleven, and had earned a doctorate from Harvard by the time he was eighteen.

Was the genius of Goethe, Wordsworth, W.B.Yeats, Henry Ford, Walt Whitman, Shakespeare, Longfellow, or Emerson by chance or wholly biological? These geniuses believed they had lived before. Edgar Allan Poe said, "It is mere idleness to say that I had not lived before – that the soul has no previous existence." Henry David Thoreau thought that reincarnation was a deep instinct in the whole human race. Benjamin Franklin wrote of it in his epitaph:

The body of B. Franklin,
Printer,
Like the Cover of an Old Book,
Its contents Torn Out
And
Stripped of its Lettering and Gilding,

Lies Here
Food for Worms,
But the Work shall not be Lost,
For it Will as he Believed
Appear Once More
In a New and more Elegant Edition
Revised and Corrected
By the Author.

"After all," mused Voltaire, "It is no more surprising to be born twice than it is to be born once."

Hard Questions

If, as we have been taught in the West, God is all-good, all-merciful, and all-loving, and gives us only one life to live, why would God create one soul a genius and the next soul an imbecile? Why would God create one soul a natural athlete and give the other a physical handicap, or create one soul to starve to death and another soul to have plenty to eat? Mozart composed symphonies prior to his seventh year. Retarded Mark Drake lay prone in a crib for thirty years. Michael Jordan is born with superior athletic ability, Stephen Moore-with Cerebral Palsy. Susan is born to the arms of loving parents while Martha is brutally battered by her father. Paul is born gay and John is born straight.

We can skirt the answer to these perplexing questions by reiterating the old adage: "You must have faith, God works in mysterious ways." Or we can take a more cynical stand that God has favorites, or ask with Descartes if God could be an evil deceiver playing a joke on humanity. But what if "whatever we sow, we also reap" *is* God's law?

Consider the idiot savant, a mentally retarded person with phenomenal ability in some one field of specialization. One savant boy had a nearly perfect ear-memory for music. He could not read music, but could hear the most complex composition and reproduce it perfectly on the piano. Another was a calendar-calculator. Given the date of any year, past or future, he could tell the day of the week that date would fall. He also could tell you the list of years on which a given date, say April 4th would fall on any particular day of the week, such as Thursday. He could produce this information faster than a calculating machine. A third savant could produce detailed and highly accurate architectural drawings of professional draftsman quality after having studied a building for only a few minutes. Neither environment nor heredity can fully explain such extraordinary talent or limitation.

From the standpoint of reincarnation and karma, our present life is the result of our past thoughts, attitudes, and actions, thus the reason for sorrow and joy, pleasure and pain rests squarely on our own shoulders. We are responsible for the joys and sorrows of our individual journey. The natural athlete may have earned a superior body with flawless coordination, yet lack morals. But if karma is God's law, then this same athlete must face obstacles that will test his or her morals in this life and perhaps in several lives until he or she learns to live morally. A person with such physical handicaps as Helen Keller may have come into this life as an inspiration and light to all humanity. Of her blindness, Helen Keller said, "I can see, and that is why I can be happy, in what you call the dark, but which to me is golden. I can see a God-made world, not a man-made world." It is difficult to know why we are born with the characteristics we have, however, if the principles of karma and reincarnation are valid, we would be wise to use these qualities well.

Individual Choices

Recall the universal orchestra example? If all souls share the goal of human wholeness, and while fulfilling their unique individuality by following different paths, then we may view reincarnation as the means of transportation. Imagine that you and a friend are to meet in Zurich, Switzerland. The distance to Zurich is the same for both of you, but you must individually choose your own route. Let's say that you decide to take a ship and your friend chooses to fly on a jet airliner. Your friend should arrive in Zurich before you, but decides to stop on the way for a little sight seeing in Italy. While sight seeing, your friend meets old friends and decides to stay in Italy awhile.

When your ship docks you rent a car and drive directly to Zurich. In the meantime your friend encounters one obstacle after another and arrives in Zurich two months later. Your individual choices make the trip longer or shorter, easier or harder, pleasant or unpleasant. The choices you make may be conscious or unconscious. Events you and your friend encounter may be effects from past lives or from the present life. The choices you make now determine the events of your future. We may insist that we did not choose a particular event, it just happened, but sometimes that is the way we choose.

If our souls have yet to finish the journey to wholeness, that is a good reason for more than one human birth. Aurobindo thought that humanity must develop into something higher than it presently is. We cannot accept terrorism, war, starvation, animal cruelty, environmental pollution, bigotry, and distrust among nations as the epitome of human endeavor. Nor can we believe the soul of an addict, a criminal, or an opportunist has developed all of its emotional, mental, or spiritual possibilities.

Imagine that bookkeeper Frank Zorno embezzled funds from a bank and was never caught for his ill deed. Many people would say he got away with it. But students of reincarnation believe he does not leave the debt unpaid at death. Frank Zorno's soul will come back as a new personality in a future life and must pay the karmic debt to learn the disadvantages of dishonesty.

Our souls yearn to be pure. As Aurobindo said, "The spirit wants to go home." If we allow greed to step in the way, we continue karmic lessons until greed is no longer an obstacle to our growth. If Michelle Snow owes a debt to Arizona Public Utilities and she moves to a new location in Oklahoma, the debt follows her. The same holds true for the reincarnating soul. If we die owing a moral debt, we come back again and again until the lesson is learned. However, if we die having lived a life of morality and goodwill, we also reap the joy of our goodwill.

Personality

We have seen that the ego both helps and hinders the progress of the soul. The ego tends to identify with a particular role in our lives that we like: the accomplished professional, the artist, icon of good works, intellectual, or the daring adventurer. We may think that reincarnation means keeping that same ego identity throughout each lifetime. We imagine that our personality does not change. But teachers of reincarnation say this is not the case. In each life we develop a different ego and a modified personality. Highly developed tendencies such as love of music, kindness, or a unique talent may prevail from life to life, but the ego is more involved with "me first" living than with spirituality. If our ego in this life were the same as our ego in past lives, we would be like robots on a treadmill. Nothing could change because the same ego in this life would have to experience the same events in every life. Thus, meaningful aspects of our personality stay with the soul, but not surface ones. Throughout the soul's journey, we adjust our personalities to deal with new situations. Experience of myriad personalities doesn't mean we have no central self-identity. We are more than the ego – we are individuals. We may say that the personal ego we develop in each life is the necessary instrument for action in that particular life.

The popular idea is that Julius Caesar is born again as John Jones, a man with the same personality, character, and attainments he had in his former life. The only difference is that he wears coat and trousers instead of a toga and speaks English instead of Latin. But repeating the same personality would have no advantage, because there would be no progress of the soul. The soul comes into birth for experience, for growth, for evolution until it is able to bring the divinity (spirit) into matter. According to rebirth philosophers, it is the true individual soul that reincarnates, and not the outer personality. The personality is simply a mold that it creates for its experiences in that one life. In another birth the soul will create a different life and career. Suppose Roman Emperor Marcus Aurelius is born again: he may be a leader, but will he be an emperor and military general or write literature that he wanted to write, but did not succeed? In another birth he may not be a ruler at all, but a poet or a yogi seeking to attain and express the highest truth. That too may have been an unrealized trend of his deeper consciousness.

In one or more lives, General Patton may be a military leader and spend his adult life planning field strategies, giving orders to subordinates and commanding military posts. The next life he may need to experience the peaceful life of a country farmer, close to the land, far removed from thoughts of war. However, if the farmers are not treated fairly, he may call upon his past leadership ability to fight for justice. Leadership ability as part of his unique individuality is not lost. In a future life, he may be a corporate executive, an astronaut, or president. Each life will add some aspect to his wholeness, yet no one life is his total soul. He could never say, "I am General Patton and nothing more."

Expressions of the Soul

Both our personality and our physical body are expressions of the soul, but not the whole soul. Our body, mind, and emotions are all molded according to the way we treated them in past lives. If we were extremely intelligent, but refused to use the rational mind and concentrated on building muscles for the "body beautiful," we could reap the results of neglecting the mind. And visa versa. If we neglect a healthy body to exercise the intellect for scholarly recognition, we would also reap the results. In the Wisdom literature of the Bible, Solomon said, "Now I was a child good by nature, and a good soul fell to my lot. Nay, rather, being good, I came into a body undefiled" (Wisdom 8: 19-20).

Philosophers of reincarnation maintain that our mental, emotional, moral, and physical attitudes will follow us until perfected. A sharp intellect used with cruel cunning must some time be tempered with kindness. The tongue can "kill" as swiftly as the bullet. Eventually the pseudo do-gooder will have to learn sincerity. Society may be convinced that the altruist is beyond selfishness, but the altruist's soul knows his or her real intentions.

Eastern philosophers as well as Western philosophers of rebirth, teach that the soul creates a new physical body to wear like a suit of clothes each lifetime. As the soul progresses through the ages, so does the physical body. From this point of view, time takes on a new meaning. What seems like a long time to us may be a minute period of time to the soul. Today the human body is different in stature than it was fifty thousand years ago. We have greater brain capacity, stand straighter, and have less body hair. As the soul grows toward spiritual consciousness, so does the physical body. Perhaps the resurrected body of Jesus the Christ is an example of what the human body can eventually become.

Reincarnation in the Judeo-Christian Tradition

We know many of the ancient Jews affirmed the truth of reincarnation. Did Jesus also believe in it? Before Jesus was born, the Jews expected the reincarnation of their great prophets. They believed Moses was Abel, the son of Adam, and they believed that the Messiah was to be the reincarnation of Adam, who had already, according to some, been born again as David. The Hebrew Bible closes with a prophecy: "Lo, I will send you Elijah, the prophet, before the day of the LORD comes…" (Malachi 3: 24). When Jesus came to the neighborhood of Caesarea Philippi, he asked his disciples, "Who do people say that the Son of Man is?" They replied, "Some say John the Baptizer, others Elijah, still others Jeremiah or one of the prophets" (Matt. 16: 13-14).

"On another occasion, Jesus' disciples asked him, 'Why do the scribes claim that Elijah must come first?' In reply, Jesus said, 'Elijah is indeed coming, and he will restore everything. I assure you, 'though, that Elijah has already come, but they did not recognize him and they did as they pleased with him. The Son of Man will suffer at their hands in the same way.' The disciples then realized that he had been speaking to them about John the Baptizer" (Matt. 17: 10-13).

Again Jesus said, "I solemnly assure you, history has not known a man born of woman greater than John the Baptizer… If you are prepared to accept it, he is Elijah, the one who was certain to come. Heed carefully what you hear!" (Matt.11: 11, 14). The testimony is repeated in Mark 9: 13: "Let me assure you, Elijah has already come. They did entirely as they pleased with him, as the Scriptures say of him."

It appears that Jesus and his disciples accepted the notion of reincarnation. In fact, Christians accepted the doctrine of reincarnation for more than five hundred years before the Byzantine Emperor Justinian declared war against the doctrine. Emperor Justinian had good reason. When people believe in reincarnation, they take personal responsibility for their present life and what happens to them in the future. That gave the church less authority and less control over their present lives. If one believes in reincarnation, the church cannot dictate to the people what happens to them after death. If there is no reincarnation, the people must surrender to church authority or suffer possible excommunication – the pain of eternal damnation.

In 553 C.E., Emperor Justinian called the Fifth Ecumenical Council together and damned the doctrine of reincarnation. Interestingly, Pope Vigilius did not attend the council meeting. Today, nearly fifteen hundred years later, a growing number of Christian clergy are suggesting that reincarnation is the "lost cord of Christianity."

Early Christians may have taken the doctrine of reincarnation for granted. It was not treated in the gospels as a new teaching or as an old one to be disavowed. For instance, "As he [Jesus] walked along he saw a man who had been blind from birth. His disciples asked him, 'Rabbi, was it his sin or that of his parents that caused him to be born blind?'" If the disciples were not speaking of reincarnation, would they have asked if the man had sinned before his own birth? Jesus was not shocked into laying down an eleventh commandment. "I say to you, Thou shalt not believe in reincarnation." He simply answered their question.

Past Life Memory

The intelligent person wants life to make sense. The idea of reincarnation helps. Imagine a person so immerged in the world of money and politics that the spiritual life was of no importance to him or her dies. Could such a person with no experience of a spiritual environment be happy on a spiritual plane? Wouldn't it be like forcing a rock music fan into an everlasting Bach concert? If an individual argues that we can learn about the spiritual life after death, then why bother with life on earth? It makes more sense to see suffering and happiness, misfortune and prosperity as experiences of the soul in training. We need not think that adversity is a punishment for some dreadful sin -- it may be a reward to moral virtue and the greatest help to the soul that is struggling to grow. On a more universal level, it may be of help to all humankind. Success, wealth, and power may be useful props if we seek them for the benefit of the planet, or they may be obstacles if we desire them for our own selfish ambition.

Some skeptics ask if reincarnation is a fact, why don't we remember past lives? Good question. The answer most teachers of reincarnation give is that we don't consciously remember past lives because we form a new personality and ego with each life. The ego-personality doesn't remember because it deals almost entirely with the world at hand. Actually, we seldom remember certain events even in this life. Do you remember being born? No, but you surely don't doubt it. Do you remember your fifth birthday? Do you remember what you had to eat last Wednesday for dinner? We don't remember many things that had to do with daily activities or with our thoughts.

In reincarnation, it is not the personality that is of the first importance, but the unique individual – the soul. When the soul departs from the physical body, shedding even the surface mental and emotions on its way, it carries with it the core of its experiences. It does not carry the physical events, emotions, mental structures, or personality, yet something essential is gathered from all of these. Such essential impressions develop the unique person that helps in the growth of the soul toward the Divine. For this reason there is usually no or very little memory of the outward events and circumstances of past lives. To recall this memory there must be a strong development of the mind, the feelings, and even the physical. For example, the essential element in the soldier – his/her loyalty, nobility, and courage – is the divine element that would express itself in the soul's character in future lives, not the uniform s/he wore.

However, something in us remembers because of the inclinations and abilities we bring with us. And some people remember past lives in very specific ways. In Sri Lanka were twin Buddhist boys that had an unusual talent for chanting extremely complex Sanskrit rituals. Both boys remembered having been Tibetan monks who had studied Sanskrit and who were killed in a bus crash. General George Patton remembered being a soldier on the battlefield. The Buddha spoke of many of his past lives. Yogis often recount past-life experiences. Professor Ian Stevenson, M.D. has investigated cases of rebirth memories. He found that children who mention rebirth usually mention it between the ages of 2-5 years. In later years an unexpected event may trigger a past life recollection.

Life's Purpose

Some people find reincarnation appealing because of the effectiveness with which it explains the purpose of life. Is one lifetime enough to experience the full range of joy, sorrow, knowledge, wisdom, and love that life has to offer? Repeated lives on earth give all humankind the opportunity to develop their full potential. Reincarnation explains many of life's puzzles. We want life to make sense. If every birth into the world is a brand new soul full of original sin, or a blank tablet, how could much progress be made? Wouldn't it be like the blind leading the blind? We would seem to need some previous experience to relate to important inner things such as love of truth, beauty, and goodness. A new soul must start from scratch. The world needs "old souls" with wisdom in outward circumstances and the innermost things of the heart to guide younger souls. It is doubtful that this kind of wisdom could be accomplished in the short span of one life.

Reincarnation gives us the opportunity to try, try again, with the assurance that each sincere effort will benefit the soul. Each time even one soul reaches a new level of spiritual consciousness it brings the world a message of hope and joy. It makes life a significant ascension by opening to us the divine vistas of a growing soul. It sets us seeking, and with a sure promise that some day we will know without the shadow of a doubt the meaning and purpose of our life on this planet.

Chapter Eight

Creation? Evolution? or Both?

*The affirmation of a divine life upon earth and an
immortal sense in a mortal existence
can have no base unless we recognize
not only eternal Spirit as the inhabitant
of this bodily mansion... but accept
Matter... as a fit and noble material out of
which He weaves constantly His garbs,
builds recurrently the unending series
of his mansions.*

Sri Aurobindo

In the Beginning

*O*ne of the strongest disagreements between scientific materialism and Christian Fundamentalism today is the theory of evolution versus the theory of creation. Scientific materialism asserts that anthropological findings and biological facts verify that humankind is the result of millions of years of evolution – from the simplest fish to the complex philosopher. Some natural scientists believe that the monkey was a kind of experimental laboratory in which nature worked out human beings.

In opposition to theories of evolution and anthropological findings, Christian fundamentalists argue that a literal reading of the bible will verify that God created human beings as humans to be humans. They believe since God created us in His image we cannot be related to the fish or the ape. Adam and Eve, the first flesh and bone human beings, literally looked just like you and me, not like Cro-Magnon or other primitive peoples. As Adam and Eve were in their days on earth, we are now, with one exception – by believing in Jesus Christ, we can be saved. For the fundamentalists, the theory of evolution is a false interpretation of anthropological findings. Based on the above viewpoints of natural science (materialism) and Christian fundamentalism, these views cannot be reconciled.

A New Set of Lenses

German philosopher Immanuel Kant would say both the materialists and the fundamentalists see the world through different sets of lenses. Today, we are developing an even clearer lens through which to view the world. By integrating traditional views of mystics, sages, and philosophers with the findings of the "new physics," no longer is the story of humankind limited to scientific observation or a literal rendering of scripture. Indeed, another picture develops. Just as scientific observation and interpreting the Bible as historical fact rely on the five senses and the analytic mind, there is another faculty that may give us greater insight into the mystery of the universe. Some of the pioneering philosophers, psychologists, and physicists of the twentieth and twenty-first century believe that a deeper meaning of both evolution and of the Bible can be found through the faculty of *intuition*. These pioneers have developed a theory that the ongoing process of change is the evolution of consciousness.

Evolution of Consciousness

The evolution of consciousness is not identical with a scientific theory of physical evolution, or with a literal interpretation of the Bible. It may accept the scientific account of biological evolution as a support, but only as a support. The materialistic theory is concerned with the outward and visible machinery and process – with nature's physical development of life and mind in matter. The evolution of consciousness, which Sri Aurobindo and others call spiritual evolution, views evolution as a progression of the soul in material existence. Aurobindo suggests that before evolution could occur there must be an involution (descent) of the Divine Spirit into matter: "In the beginning God created the heaven and the earth. And the earth was without form and void; and darkness was upon the face of the deep. And the Spirit of God moved upon the face of the waters" (Gen. 1: 1-2). Without the Divine Spirit descending into matter, there would be no evolution (ascent) but a successive creation of new things purely by random chance.

Aurobindo discovered that all growth is the evolution of consciousness – an integral part of the creation connecting humankind with all life. Today, philosophers, mystics, and some physicists interchange the word consciousness with the word spirit. If the world and everything in it is an evolution of consciousness, then evolution is spiritual as well as biological and in no way contradicts either natural science or the meaning of scripture.

For instance, "In the beginning when God created heaven and earth..." may mean that within heaven and earth exists the potential for all created things to reach their final goal. The meaning here would be different than the belief that God created everything in heaven and earth as finished and unchanging products. However, we do see changes occurring throughout time. At first the human species had a collective sense of self that was hardly differentiated from the natural world. They lived much like a herd or a flock and this sense of a collective self lasted for millions of years.

Human Development

As the evolution of consciousness progressed, human beings focused more on the clan or family. Gradually our ancestors were no longer ape-men but tribal Neanderthal humans who clearly differentiated themselves from nature. With the emergence of the Cro-Magnon people, a sense of personal identity emerged for the first time in human history. Cro-Magnon was not biologically very different from Neanderthal, but in their mentality there was a "change in consciousness." A new state of consciousness marked their emergence. They buried their dead in graves with funerary objects near the bodies, thus demonstrating a sense of soul and afterlife. Cro-Magnon had a sense of personal individuality and their funeral rites showed that they believed that personality continued after death.

Over vast epochs of time, consciousness emerged in a stronger ever more individualized sense of self in the human species. This state of consciousness in the human race brought with it new mental powers. By the time of the

Neolithic Age, humans had developed an "ego." This was when the first heroes of humanity arose – those who took control of their lives. This period of development set the stage for another change in human consciousness. However, as we know, the analytic mind and the ego cause our sense of separateness, thus people were inherently unhappy because the ego is incomplete and cut off from wholeness and harmony with the cosmos. However the analytic mind with its ego isn't our highest faculty. The faculty of intuition (only dimly developed in most) leads us to higher consciousness that transcends the ego of separateness (see Ch. 9). Such consciousness has been displayed in rare individuals such as Socrates, Jesus, Buddha, Aurobindo, Eckhart and others.

God's Design

According to Aurobindo, the evolution of consciousness is the Divine intelligence at work. It is present in everything from the simplest sub-atomic particle to the most complex human genius. God is involved in a creative process that begins in material unconsciousness and ends in spiritual consciousness. As the psalmist said, "Even in the midst of hell there are Thou also." So if war is hell, God is also present there. Perhaps all things work for the good of humanity, even war. The divinity is in everything... "Even with the dove that falls." We reach the ultimate wholeness only after we experience the various levels and combinations needed to understand the meaning of our relationship to God and the universe.

Creation in Progress

At our level of consciousness we have yet to identify with the divinity in the way Jesus did: "I and the Father are one." And he added: "As I am so can you be." However, as a baby must grow through childhood and teenage years before reaching adulthood, we too must transcend the imperfections in our physical bodies, emotional attitudes, and mental thinking to become more spiritual and intuitive human beings. Philosopher Teilhard de Chardin thought the seven days of creation is still in process. Our present stage is *Noogenesis,* the mind and ego consciousness. The next stage in evolution, he said, will be *Christogenesis* – a transformation of the ego mentality into the harmony of unconditional love.

If Teilhard de Chardin and others are correct and consciousness is the basis of the universe, then evolution is still in process and the days of creation as written in Genesis are actually Great Ages. One of God's days could equal hundreds, thousands, or millions of years. The word "day" may be the symbol of a greater time period such as an Age or Eon. Could "The seventh day God rested" refer to the future Golden Age when all human souls reach unconditional love and truth? Could the process possibly stop before the kingdom of heaven is realized on earth? Are we presently striving to reach the Golden Age, but not quite adult or mature enough to achieve it?

The analogy of baking bread may best explain creation in progress. First, the baker (God) imagines the finished product then mixes the ingredients, one by one. Once the bread attains a particular texture, the baker kneads together (the process of creation) the ingredients. After kneading the dough, the baker places it into a bowl to rise. After the rising process, the dough is punched down, shaped into individual loaves, and placed into bread pans to rise again. At the appropriate time, the loaves are placed into the oven to bake. Each step must be taken, and no ingredient can be substituted if the process is to work. The recipe itself would be the blueprint in the mind of God. If we liken the Book of Genesis to the bread recipe, we see that the world contains all the necessary ingredients for the finished product, but the finished product doesn't appear until all the essential steps are taken. Could it be that we humans, and everything in creation, are baking in the world oven, but not quite done?

Teilhard de Chardin thought that we are teenagers in a maturing universe learning to become adults (Christ-like). Our opinions often lack knowledge. Nations disagree about the role government should play. Religions stand in opposition concerning the nature of God, humankind, and morality. Public opinion differs with regard to TV programs, cars, clothes, music, sports, computers, lifestyles, politics, retirement, and where to vacation. In the face of what Krishna, the Buddha, Lao Tzu, Confucius, Zoroaster, Moses, Jesus, Muhammad and other great spiritual leaders have taught, we in our immaturity (ignorance) turn away from the spiritual life to satisfy selfish ego desires. "Forgive them" Jesus said. "They know not what they do."

We think we know exactly what we do and why we do it – but do we? We quote scripture, but do we take it to heart? Engraved on the penny is *"In God we Trust."* But do we trust God or do we rely on the economy? In his book, *World Religions*, Huston Smith alluded to the difficulties the world has with the "Good News" Jesus gave us. We are told to love our enemies and bless them that curse us. But the world teaches us to hate our enemies and repay forcefully those that persecute us. Jesus instructed people to resist no evil – to turn the other cheek. The world assumes evil must be fought in every conceivable way. Like a tornado, evil uproots anything in its path unless nothing lies in its path to unearth. Evil gives strength only to that which resists it. As the Buddha said, "Evil never ceases by evil alone, evil ceases by love."

Huston Smith addressed other examples: Jesus taught us to be as carefree as birds of the air and lilies of the field, but the world, in its fear, advises us to build our economic security through defense for the nation and insurance for individuals, now and for the future. According to the gospels, it is wrong to judge others, but the world assumes religions, governments, and educational systems other than our own, are false. We are taught in scripture that the happy people are the meek and pure in heart. The world, in its ignorance, assumes that happiness belongs to the rich, the famous and powerful individuals. We are told to give freely, but we expect tax receipts, recognition, or praise for our efforts. Jesus emphasized that the path to salvation is straight and narrow. The world, grasping for security, follows the curves of conformity and convention.

Obviously, we have a long road to travel before we, in the light of Jesus' teachings, can be the bearers of the "Good News." We do not want to be bad or ignorant. We try to be good. We think our actions are right actions. However, if we take a closer look, aren't we acting like imperfect, immature people with a huge dose of ego? If evolution is the growth of consciousness, then as we evolve into higher states of spiritual awareness, we intuitively distinguish the selfishness in ourselves from the unselfishness. We could consider our growth through the process of evolution as a self-unfolding – trimming away the chaff from the wheat. As we evolve it may be easier to distinguish the chaff from the wheat in our daily lives.

INVOLUTION AND EVOLUTION

Let's return to the creative process. Aurobindo called evolution the *ascent* of matter, life, and mind to the true home in the spirit. He considered evolution a growth out of unconsciousness and ignorance into conscious awareness. Before evolution could begin, there had to be an involution or *descent* of spirit into matter, life, and mind. The involution of God's presence in the world makes the world holy. Recall Genesis 1: 2, "...the earth was a formless wasteland and darkness covered the abyss..." Darkness could be the symbol for unconscious chaos (no/thing, no/form). "Then God said, 'Let there be light, and there was light'" (Gen. 1: 3). Light could be the symbol for spiritual truth. According to the *involution/ evolution* theory, when God sent a stream of light (spirit) into the darkness, the seed of the universe was planted. The intelligent spirit of God existing within the seed caused it to move and at that moment Time was created.

Without the divine intelligence in them, atoms and molecules would not know what function to perform. All things follow a pattern that scientists call natural law: Atoms come together to form a molecule; hydrogen and oxygen unite to make water. In the evolution of consciousness schema, natural law is the result of the divine intelligence in nature. Like computers, elements are programmed by the Supreme intelligence to perform in certain ways. Hydrogen and oxygen always make water, never carrot juice. God propels atoms to act as atoms and cells to perform as cells; plants to absorb water through their roots; animals to eat, sleep, and procreate; humans to reflect and ask questions. The divine consciousness is the foundation for all evolution and is everywhere present.

Father Bede Griffiths wrote, "The whole world is a sign of this Mystery, from Brahman [God] to a blade of grass. It is everywhere and nowhere. Everything speaks of it – the evil as well as the good, the pain and mystery of life as well as the joy and beauty – but it remains hidden." Using poetic language, we could, in the words of William Blake, "See the world in a grain of sand."

According to the evolution of consciousness theory, evolution is "God's on-going creation." Matter carries within itself the potential for life, because the principle of life is from the beginning involved in matter. But life cannot burst forth until matter has developed the right conditions to give birth to the cell. When the cell is born, life can begin on earth. In the first cell lies the mystery of all future life varieties, just as in the acorn is the mystery of the future oak tree. The mature oak tree cannot burst all of a sudden and fully grown from the tiny acorn, it needs to follow the process of natural law. First the acorn is planted in suitable soil, then rain, sun, and cool weather, help it germinate. At the right time, known only to acorn consciousness, it bursts open and the first tender oak shoot pops up through the earth. In spring and summer it grows and in the fall and winter it rests. Soon the shoot grows into a sapling, and from the sapling evolves the mature oak tree. How does the acorn know what to do? The Divine intelligence is present in it. Just as a computer programmer programs a computer, God programs the universe, only on a much grander scale.

Like the acorn, various levels of life evolve. In higher forms of animal life we see the first glimmerings of mind, but before reflective mind can function properly there must evolve a brain that is complex enough to be its instrument.

Here, the point of departure occurs between natural scientists that posit a biological evolution based on the "survival of the fittest," and consciousness evolutionists that posit a God-directed evolution. Scientific materialists locate the human mind in the physical brain. Consciousness evolutionists view the physical brain as an instrument of the mind. They assert that humans are more than a physical body, consisting of subtle fields of consciousness the naked eye cannot see. Thus mind exists in a more ethereal realm than the visible human brain. If the mind were wholly physical, how could it conceptualize, grasp abstract thoughts, or reflect on God?

According to Aurobindo the spirit directs each step of the evolution and every step is a spiral upward. The first step is the evolution of matter out of the nescience (darkness). The involution into nescience pushes the evolution upward resulting in organized matter in which each atom holds infinite potential energy. The second step in evolution is life. As matter evolves into life, it does not reject its old basis, rather new impulses appear that were implanted in it. Each cell or unit of life holds within itself the potential power of becoming. The third step is the evolution of mind. With mind in humanity came the mental or intellectual consciousness. Mind does not leave matter and life behind, but assimilates both. In fact, the mind helps govern matter and life. With mind comes the question: Who am I? When mind comes into play, humanity becomes aware of its limitations and that is why Aurobindo said, "Man is the greatest of living beings because he is the most discontented, because he feels most the pressure of limitations."

Levels of Consciousness

According to the evolution of consciousness, the human body evolved through all the necessary levels of nature until its brain was sufficiently developed to act as an instrument for the faculty of reason. With the involution of the rational mind, human beings were born. When the spirit descended into dark matter, mind was asleep within spirit and it slept until matter and life developed an instrument suitable for mind to operate. Thus the more we evolve the more fully the mind wakes up. Involution and evolution always work together.

Accordingly, our physical bodies are the result of millions of years of God's creative act directing nature from mineral to plant to animal to human. Today human bodies continue to share certain animal characteristics: we eat, eliminate, nurse our young, fight or flee, protect our territory, procreate, drink water, seek shelter, sleep, and dream. More than two thousand years ago the Greek philosopher Aristotle observed that the problem of human *morality* arises from the conflicts between our animal nature and our rational mind. Such conflicts cause societies to develop moral laws to upgrade human behavior. Animal instincts urge survival of the fittest; if one animal has food another may try to snatch it. Human reason realizes that in a moral society we should not steal from each other. Individuals that allow animal instincts to overrule reason are threats to society and we lock them up.

Raising us beyond the instinctual animal level, reason offers an opportunity to reach beyond our immediate personal environment to responsible moral living. Through the use of intellect, we take it upon ourselves to understand other cultures, causes of disease, outer space, technology, and business techniques. But is reason the highest faculty of the mind? Can reason answer the questions: Who am I? What if anything is the destiny of humankind? If reason or intellect were the highest faculty of knowledge, wouldn't all rational people agree on such subjects as: the purpose of the universe, human morality, religion, foreign trade, and politics?

The closer we look, the more evidence presents itself that the mind has several levels of consciousness. The physical level is most active in people who believe material objects as money, houses, cars, food, and entertainment will make them happy. Recalling Plato's theory of the soul, we find people on the next level seeking happiness through success, power, adventure, fame, respect, and fighting for important causes. On the reasoning level we hope to find happiness in analyzing ideas and solving problems in the arts and sciences. But no matter how well we use the intellect, we find ourselves stuck in moral and religious conflict. We help a friend and declare war on an enemy. We lend nations economic support and turn against them in aggression. The ego grows strong and we feel isolated from our own and other species. And the soul continues to be dissatisfied.

Carl G. Jung would agree with Theosophy, Teilhard de Chardin, Henri Bergson, Aurobindo and others that the intuitive faculty is the next step in our evolution of consciousness. The intuitive faculty has direct accessibility to universal truth via spiritual insight. Mystics of all religions agree that at a high level of intuition we understand God's meaning. That is the significance of reaching the *Christogenesis* stage of consciousness in Teilhard's schema. After St. Paul's revelation to surrender his own ego to the Christ, he proclaimed, "Not I who live, but Christ lives in me." Just one drop of God's splendor changes our outlook on life.

The Buddha said of himself: "I am awake." Enlightenment means to "wake up." Following his realization the Buddha felt the need to share his spiritual findings with the five ascetics with whom he had practiced bodily disciplines so severe that he often fainted from lack of food. They had hoped to break from the physical body into spiritual enlightenment, but so far had not succeeded. The Buddha had wondered if a better method could be found, and one day he left the five ascetics to continue his search alone. Now the awakened Buddha wished to share his spiritual insights with them. As he approached, the five ascetics turned away with contempt: "Here comes the prince who refused to discipline his body. We shall neither rise to meet him nor offer him a place to sit." However, as the Buddha approached, such pure love flowed from him that the five ascetics broke their resolve. They bowed before the enlightened Buddha and offered him a seat. After teaching them of the Middle Path in which one neither gives in to pleasure or tortures the body, the five became his disciples.

Whether Christian, Buddhist, Hindu, Taoist, Muslim, Jew, or independent, unconditional love flows from the awakened into the world. Enlightened beings are free of judgment and emotional attachment. Their souls have awakened to the true meaning of life. For individuals who believe in the evolution of consciousness, "waking-up" is the goal. When we reach this stage by developing our intuition, we live fully the divine life and experience the universe and everything in it as an expression of God's joy.

The road isn't easy, nor can we truly understand "unconditional love" by reading love poetry, watching late night TV romantic movies, or absorbing ourselves in amorous novels. We must experience love in our own lives. To understand the meaning of love on any level – romantic love, love of nature, a pet, a child, a friend, humanity, or God – we need to be involved in the loving process. Through intuition we may be confident that a divine intelligence is at work in our lives, individually and collectively. And although we have free will to resist the call to wholeness and love, that call cannot be resisted forever. Preparing ourselves is a long, arduous journey toward deeper realization of unity that includes the cosmic, biological, and social systems. This remarkable interrelationship reminds us of St. Paul's words: "We are all members of one another."

Chapter Nine

Higher Consciousness

There is a limit where the intellect
  fails and breaks down, and this limit
  is where the questions concerning God,
  and freewill, and immortality arise.

Immanuel Kant

Adventure of Consciousness

*T*oday, as never before in history, we live in the age of the global community. With the awesome advances in information technology, we can know in minutes what is happening all over the world. Thus, many people believe that the solution to the world's problems rests squarely on the shoulders of science and technology. Technology and new findings in science have influenced the job market, international communication, and the future economy. The social sciences have done much to inform us about populations, economic behavior, and changes in customs. We know more than ever before about the varieties of societies throughout the world. We can surf the Internet for Bed and Breakfasts, plane fares, and interesting events taking place all over the world.

But have the areas of computer technology, space exploration, or electronic communications influenced our understanding of what reality is? Can they even begin to tell us what it means to be human, what life and death are, what moral responsibility is, or what a nurturing environment for the future of the planet is? Science informs us of what means to take to what ends. But, can science tell us about ends themselves? Science tells us how people *do* behave and how societies *are* organized. But can science tell us how people *ought* to behave and how societies *ought* to be organized?

Science can no more tell us what human nature is than the map of Arizona can explain the mystery of its amazing deserts and canyons. The map is simply something useful when we need to find our way about.

Mystics tell us there is another way of looking at the world and ourselves that gives us deeper insight into our true nature. William James had the experience that our world of waking consciousness is a kind of veil behind which the true business of reality is going on. With James, some of us have experienced this insight in some degree, but the great mystics of all ages have had it in the highest degree. By penetrating the veil behind the maps of natural science, the saints, sages, and shamans of all traditions have experienced the true nature of reality. Most have called this reality God and they agree that the best description of this reality is unconditional love. Such an insight into the nature of reality is also an insight into our human nature and into the world as a whole. These adventurers of consciousness recognize all things as expressions of the divine – the warp and woof of the world is the kinship of all life.

According to some brain researchers, thinking is an activity of the left brain and intuition an activity of the right brain. More recently scientists have discovered that the brain is like a hologram and memory is not located in one part of the brain but is present throughout the brain. Karl Pribram, a professor of neurophychology at Stanford University was the first to formulate a holographic theory of the brain. He found that the brain as a hologram mirrored information in every part rather than storing it in a particular area. Thus we have immediate intuitive access that does not require a chain reaction transmitting information from one neuron to another until we are conscious of the information. Physicist David Bohm found that awareness is woven throughout this holographic structure. "Deep down the consciousness of mankind is one."

The World of Contrasts

The holographic theory suggests that we have the ability to

recognize unity within the deep source of reality, because this knowledge dwells innately in each of us. Yet we tend to view the world and each other as separate entities. Although the mystics and the new physicists have found that everything in the world is interrelated, we continue to act out of our dual nature. We save lives and destroy lives both physically and psychologically. We relish the earth and litter the earth. We show kindness to our co-workers and renounce them for our own ambition. We tell the truth and we lie. We love and we hate. Our way of thinking divides everything into parts. We continue to experience the mind, spirit, and body as three different parts of ourselves. Seldom do we perceive ourselves as whole and integrated beings.

Through dualism we live in a contrasted world of light and darkness. We divide existence into pure and impure or good and evil. We see God as above and the devil as below. In the West, dualism divides humankind, the world, and the Godhead into upper and lower – mind and body, heaven and hell, God and the devil, and spirit and matter. The ideal figure of a dualistic view is the *hero* who takes the form of a *saint* that we consider identical with the principle of good (symbolized by the halo), or someone like Saint Gregory subduing the dragon (lower nature). The lower, darker side is always defeated and excluded from life.

Such duality is in the heart of each of us. We are soul and body. We are reason and appetite. We are angel and devil. We are at war with ourselves. Isn't it fascinating that our human species can include such opposing specimens as Christ and Caesar, the Buddha and Genghis Khan, Gandhi and Hitler? Rather than judge these seeming opposites as good and bad, the duality here might be less between good and evil than between ways of viewing the world.

If we are to understand others (and we must if we want others to understand us) it seems crucial to see that the destroyers of history have not characteristically acted out of wickedness. They thought what they were doing was right. They believed it was for the good of humanity or for the glory of God that certain people and nations had to be oppressed and destroyed. This conflict between loving the "enemy" and hating the "enemy" is generally, if not universally, found in each of us.

Can science and technology tell us if there is or is not an absolute standard of right and wrong? For such information, we turn to philosophers and theologians. Socrates and Plato believed in an absolute standard of *Truth, Beauty,* and *Goodness.* They also argued that these principles transcend the standards of conventional society. In other words the principles of truth, beauty, and goodness are not subject to time/space, therefore they cannot be found in the world of change – the phenomenal world. Only the soul is able to relate to these eternal verities, so to know them we must look within. Once we know truth, beauty, and goodness, society's morality seems to pale, and if we are true to ourselves we aspire to heed the higher law. By following such lofty principles, the Athenians put Socrates to death and the Jews and Romans crucified Jesus. Societies have judged Gandhi, William Blake, Martin Luther King, Walt Whitman, Fredrick Nietzsche, H.P. Blavatsky, and just about every individual whose creativity soared beyond the confines of conventional morality.

Rules of Society

French philosopher Henri Bergson asserted that like the ants and the bees, humans are social beings, and like ants and bees our chief instrument for survival is social organization. As a species, we are relatively weak physically and have a perilously long childhood. We are, above all else, tool users and these tools can be most effectively used when there is a division of labor in exchange of goods and services. Thus, we can survive only with social cooperation. Of course, as we have seen through history, such cooperation must be structured by rules in a framework of a social institution. And for the social institution to survive, we must conform to the rules.

As it is an instinct in the bees and ants to conform to the rules of the hive and of the hill, Bergson found that humans have also an instinct to conform to the rules of society. Unlike the ants and bees, we use our ego and intellect to determine the particular circumstances of our society. The importance of ego and intellect cannot be overstated as instruments for our survival. In fact, Bergson observed, the intellect far surpasses in its subtlety any of the technological instruments we have produced. The ego is the authority that meets the demands of society and rejects anything contrary to its approval. Above all else, the ego wants to survive.

Although rules may vary from society to society, the principle behind the rules is the same everywhere: "You shall do what your society commands." These basic instincts are so powerful that we feel compelled to obey them because of the pressure of our conscience. We may groan and complain when rules of society change, but we obey most of them. One of the most powerful changes was racial prejudice and affirmative action. Another change was of policy in institutions of higher education toward hiring gays and lesbians. Not so long ago in Puritanical America it was a sin to go to the theater, to date without a chaperon, to ride on a train or bus, to wear skimpy clothing, or to stay away from church.

Because the purpose of any social order is that its members endure, it needs strict organization and authority. The problem is that a society with exacting standards becomes as inflexible as the society of the ants or the bees. To keep society uniform, unique and creative individuals are stifled. Although different cultures hold different things to be taboo, the fact remains that all cultures have a basic standard of right and wrong.

Fixed Rules and Values

In the conventional social order there is no recognition of any obligation to all human beings. Nor is there any recognition of merely human rights. There is only the concept of those who act appropriately and those who do not, i.e., those who follow the authority of society and those who do not. People who follow fixed rules want justice and love of others, but only of others who are members of their group. It is a kind of justice and love that is compatible with injustice and hatred.

Conventionalized values show themselves in times of stress when the group is in danger or thinks that it is in danger. The Baptist Church boycotted Disney Studios for giving gay and lesbian companions medical benefits. The Baptists believed that by acknowledging the union of gays and lesbians, Disney was breaking the rules of conventional morality, thus corrupting their group. One of the prominent fundamentalist Christian leaders announced that terrible floods, earthquakes, and hurricanes would hit Orlando, Florida because of Disney's acceptance of gays and lesbians as domestic partners. We know that some of the artists and creators of Disney World entertainment are gays and lesbians. So long as the fact was hidden, anti-gay and lesbian groups happily attended Disney World. But once the fact became public, the creators of their entertainment suddenly turned to monsters. The shadow again!

Societies closed to freeing individuals to be themselves embrace the *scapegoat* mentality. Scapegoat mentality means that people with fixed unchanging standards often project their own unconscious emotions on certain "unacceptable" individuals in the outside world. To avoid confronting themselves in such guises as the beggar or cripple, the outcast or bad person, the fool the despised, or the insulted, the robber, and the addicted, they attack undesirable individuals and groups, thus eliminating their own guilt. Over two thousand years ago Hebrew tribes used the scapegoat. The tribal members would pile their sins on the goat then exile it into the desert wilderness to die. But the scapegoat mentality did not end two thousand years ago. Today society uses the scapegoat psychology to deal with those outside their group. Within our own country the people who are the objects of these projections are the minorities, new-age spirituality, the environmentalists, the animal activists, or anyone who doesn't fit the conventional moral standard. The more dogmatically the masses impose their fixed standards on individuals, the more radically they exclude them.

Fixed structures also express themselves in political parties and religion. Those who do not follow the prescribed set of dogmas, who do not participate in ritual and agree with basic doctrine, are excluded from the group. The primary focus of this type of thinking is on the stability of doctrine. Religions arrange universal spiritual truths into a set of dogmas that belong exclusively to their particular denomination. In this way dogmatic religions express the attitude of exclusivity that is found in conventional society – like the ants and the bees. The rigidity of structure demands individual conformity.

Intuition

Instinctively we all want to conform to a degree, but some of us also wish to be free. Is it possible to rise above instinct, rigid intellect, and the group mentality? Mystics and other adventurers in consciousness say yes. Within the evolving consciousness is the faculty of *intuition*. Through intuition, said Aurobindo, we experience a direct insight into reality. Through intuition we are free to develop and realize our creative capacities. When using intuition, the intellect and ego that separate one thing from the other fade into a true holistic awareness. We begin to see everyone and everything as an aspect of the divinity – humans, plants, animals, earth, seas, and celestial bodies. Intuition places no judgment on race, religion or gender. Through intuition we are able to share Walt Whitman's inner experience: "Swiftly arose and spread around me the peace of knowledge that pass all the argument of the earth." He knew he was the brother of God and that all human beings were his brothers and sisters, and that we should "...love the earth and sun and the animals..." Intuitively we behold everything and everybody as a living harmonious unity. Using the ego and intellect exclusively, we have a secure society of rules, but the center doesn't hold. To *sin* is "to miss the mark." It is not misbehavior in society, but failure to be centered in God. The ego can't help but miss the mark. With intuition, the center holds.

The faculty of reason helps us proceed to our goal step by step, by analysis and organization. The direct insight of intuition into reality skips the step-by-step procedure by reaching knowledge instantaneously. For many people intuition is frightening because they have been trained to always follow the laws of logic. They distrust the intuitive process and even if they have intuition, they try to ignore it. If one of their friends has an intuition they call it a "hunch" or "lucky guess." But according Aurobindo and Jung, intuition never contradicts the laws of logic it merely passes them over by immediately perceiving the whole picture in a flash. Jung said, "In intuition a content presents itself whole and complete, without our being able to explain or discover how this content came into existence." Aurobindo explained intuition as an opening to realization: "Intuition sees the truth of things by a direct inner contact." Philosopher Dane Rudhyar called intuition "holistic perception." For example, we know when people are honest, because honesty emanates from them. Intuition gives us direct insight. Have you ever met a person and known immediately that person had substance? Have you ever walked along with a friend and you knew she was upset even though she denied it? Or entered an unfamiliar house and at once felt at home —or just the opposite? You can't distinguish it with your senses and you can't distinguish it with your intellect – you just know.

Albert Einstein arrived at his famous theory of relativity not by cumbersome linear thought but through a flash of insight. His intuition not only went beyond the available evidence, it was not even verifiable through experiments at that time. Yet today the theory of relativity is one of the cornerstones of modern physics.

Remember the spaceship with the civilian teacher that blew up in space? The news media and NASA thought the crew had been killed instantly. An artist friend had a vision of some of the crew alive in the ocean with their space helmets on -- slowly drowning. The vision saddened her terribly and she could neither eat nor sleep. Days later the media reported that the crew had not been killed instantly after all – some had drowned.

Fashion designers are notorious for their insights into what kinds of clothes people will wear in the future. Some stockbrokers intuit tomorrow's stock market. Have you ever decided to phone a person and just before you dialed, that person called you? Have you ever had a hunch that a certain horse was going to win a race and it did? Intuition gives us these insights – if we would learn to trust it.

Intuition and creativity both bubble up from the same living spring within us. Learning to rely on intuition we would live more active, more conscious, and more creative lives. Creative individuals are the pioneers that lead humankind to higher recesses of knowledge.

Insight into Human Nature

We all have intuition in some degree, but the great mystics of all ages and places have had it in the highest degree. They all agree that reality isn't something fixed or changeless -- the world and everything in it is in process. They explain reality as spontaneous and creative, with direction. It is a process towards higher consciousness and more freedom. This insight into the nature of reality brings with it an insight into our own nature – that we are expressions of this creative force. And in discovering our ultimate nature we discover our purpose – to reach higher consciousness and thus live the divine life on earth.

When we try to think about and analyze reality, it appears fragmented. Since the nature of the intellect is to divide and separate, the reasoning faculty cannot directly understand continuity – it always tries to analyze the flowing process into parts. The picture of reality that intellect has is like a series of snapshots such as chairs, tables, people, trees, and planets. True reality, said Bergson, gives us an inner connection with self-consciousness -- a continuous flux, a succession of states with no beginning and no end. It is a process that words cannot express except to say that it includes growth, creativity, and freedom.

Just as our instincts draw us to follow conventional values, our intuition leads us into the meaning of human nature. We know intuitively that we are not only physical beings – we are beings with a mind, consciousness, and creativity. We know that we are not merely the products of our social environment, but that we are free. Whereas the social order focuses on the good of the group, intuition realizes the creative self-development of the individual. Whereas the focus of the organized intellect is the biological survival of the species, the focal point of intuition is the creative self-actualization of the individual. This spirituality is not concerned with the acceptance of dogma or ritual. It focuses on the spiritual enlightenment of the individual grounded in the mystical experiences of such individuals as Christ, Buddha, Aurobindo, Eckhart, Whitman and others.

Intuition is our inner aspiration to be true to a higher sense of self: *To thine own self be true.* When that spiritual command is denied, we feel as if we have betrayed ourselves – sold out. As Rabbi Suyas said, "In the world to come, I shall not be asked: 'Why were you not Moses?' I shall be asked: 'Why were you not Suyas?'"

The basic conflicts in our lives are between parts within us. While it often feels that we are caught between our own and another person's image of us, actually the conflict is between two desires within me: 1) my desire to be what I want to be, and 2) my desire to be what you want me to be. Perhaps that is why mythologist Joseph Campbell said again and again: "Follow your bliss."

KINSHIP OF ALL LIFE

Conforming to the rules and obligations of society may bring about a sense of self-righteous contentment, but when we close ourselves off to any but our own group's standards we fail to deal with our dark side – the shadow. If my shadow is anti-social and greedy, cruel and malicious, poor and miserable, and in a dream approaches me as a beggar, a witch, a tramp, or a wild beast, I can reconcile my shadow with the whole human race. When I intuit what is unacceptable in myself, I can accept it in my neighbor, for *I am that!* Being that, however, does not mean I must act it out. I may recognize that addiction lives in humankind and in myself. I don't have to be an alcoholic to know I wish not to be one. But I would recognize that within my being lurks the possibility of addiction. As Gandhi said: If it is not in me, how could I recognize it in someone else?

Once we come to terms with the fact that we are all interconnected it is easier to trust our intuition that every human being aspires toward higher consciousness. Ultimately, if we continue to aspire we will accept and love others as members of the great family – humankind. Love is the bond that unites all things and creatures in the world.

Intuition helps us understand the insights of the great poets, philosophers, and mystics throughout history. Although their utterances may seem extravagant, mad, and totally unintelligible, yet we can't fail to feel there is something significant and important being said by them. "I believe in you my soul," sang Walt Whitman, "loaf with me on the grass." "I am the vine, you are the branches," said Jesus. Another time he held up a piece of bread: "This is my body." Then he raised a glass of wine; "This is my blood." And St. Paul exclaimed, "Not I who lives but Christ lives in me." For T.S. Eliot, "The rose and the fire are one." Aurobindo perceived "… a divine light that leans over the world." When we encounter such words, a bell rings in us. Somewhere in our experience we know something akin to what they know.

Intuition and Divinity

Through intuition comes that essential insight into truth, beauty, and goodness. Intuitive philosophers agree that we are governed by the intelligence of the universe – by God's intelligence. And it is from the recognition of the deep source of this intuition that its authority springs. Yes, there is something in us that says, "Subordinate yourself to your group." But there is also something else that says, "Serve humankind and the planet." This latter intuition is the expression of our higher self. Our intellect says, "Help your friends and harm your enemies," but intuition replies, "Not even your enemies." And this intuition we recognize as the essence of our Divine Self.

Perhaps one of the most important evolutionary developments of history is that intuition has come into existence and some day its deep insights will replace today's conventional values. In the course of evolution the next stage could see both the intellect and intuition devoted to new ends. The ends may not be mere survival, not merely the good of the group, but devoted to bringing into existence a conscious and free humanity – a loving humanity.

It's amazing to experience those at the service of intuition. There is the artist, the philosopher, and the great moral and religious heroes of history -- as well as today's pioneering women and men. Above all, the inspiration that comes from confronting such persons is that they show their divinity. The impulse of the universe acts in and through them. If we can perceive God in the lives of the great scientists, artists, political leaders, educators, medical doctors, researchers and everyday heroes – if we can perceive God in the rocks, flowers, animals, and stars – if we can perceive God in each other – we will have awakened to the holy presence.

Chapter Ten

Religion & Spirituality

Spirituality is always outside the churches
or the temples or mosques.
Spirituality is something different
from religion.
Spirituality transcends creeds, cults,
and codes of behavior.

Beatrice Bruteau

Contributions of Religion

*B*ecause many of our needs are not met by the physical world, many people find it difficult to accept that this life is all there is. We are born, we progress from childhood to teenage to adult, we struggle to support ourselves, we age, and we die. People want some assurance that life continues beyond the grave, and they want this present life to have meaning. Religions help to uncover meaningfulness in the midst of the mundane.

Religions help us explore the *transpersonal* dimension of life – the eternal and infinite, beyond limited worldly concerns.

Thus people look to religions for understanding, for answers to our many questions about life. Who are we? Why are we here? What happens after we die? Why is there suffering? Why is there evil? Is anybody up there listening? For those who find security in specific answers, religions offer *dogma* – systems of doctrines they proclaim as absolutely true. Faith in dogma provides people with a sense of relief from anxieties and a secure feeling of roots. Religions also provide rules for living that govern everything from diet and dress to personal relationships.

ORGANIZED RELIGION

The main concern of any religion is to inspire reverence for God and to give comfort and meaning to life for a community of believers. Although some religions insist their members follow closely Church dogma, other religions encourage their members to explore the perennial questions and to live the uncertainties of not knowing intellectually. Although religions differ in their belief systems, most religions share some common ingredients:

1. *Authority.* Divine and human. The problems of people's religious life can be very complicated, so religions have advisors such as priests, ministers, and bishops. The ordained authorities interpret scripture and teach the doctrines of the religion and/or church to their lay members.

2. *Ritual.* Religion originated with celebration and consternation: joyful get-togethers that included rhythm, song and dance, and an established procedure of public worship based on a book of rites or ceremonies led by a person or persons of authority.

3. *Speculation.* Theories of God that are the basis of church dogma and doctrine. Religions have doctrines about ultimate issues – how the spiritual world is set up, what ultimate reality is, where the world and humans came from and where they are going.

4. *Tradition.* Religious beliefs, stories, and customs handed down from generation to generation. Tradition is a body of teachings and laws formulated by the founder of the religion and his or her apostles. Interpretation may differ among religions.

5. *God's sovereignty and grace.* Humankind is

dependent upon a God or gods that we did not make nor can we control. We depend upon God's gifts to human beings that make life possible and sustain it. In Christianity, for example, salvation depends not upon our own efforts, but upon God's grace.

6. *Mystery.* The unknown and unexplained, such as the Godhead and Nature. Christian mystery lies in the life of the Virgin Mary, the passion of Christ, and in the sacramental rite of the Eucharist. Some ancient religions had mystery rites and rituals known only to initiates.

7. *Community.* Religion by its very nature is social. Religion is never just an individual affair but always involves the person in a larger community of people going on that religious path. Each religion provides its members with a structure for daily life based on its particular dogma and doctrines. Within each religion exist individual denominations or sects that agree on basic principles, but not on interpretation. For example, within Christianity we have Orthodox, Roman Catholic, Baptist, Methodist, Quaker, Christian Science, LDS, and so on. Moral principles differ from denomination to denomination; it is not immoral for Roman Catholics to partake of alcohol in moderation. Baptists and Mormons (LDS) may not drink alcohol at all. However, all denominations agree on certain moral principles such as telling the truth and keeping promises.

Defining Yourself

Particularly helpful is the ability to define yourself through a specific religion. You can define the rules for belonging to that religion and in turn that religion helps define you. You can say that you are a Presbyterian or a Jew, or a Shiite, or

Pure Land Buddhist, or Baha'I, and console yourself that you know a little better who you are and where you fit into the world and even into the reality beyond the world.

Unfortunately, rather than bringing humankind together, religion tends to divide. We know that race and nationality divide people, but the greatest division lies in religion. Once you "belong" to a religion, you may feel that your religion is superior to other religions – your group superior to other groups. You may become comfortable in your beliefs of God, morality, and the afterlife. Most religions do not encourage lay people to question, inquire or to find out what is true and what is false. You should accept religious authority on faith and believe in the doctrines of your particular religion. If we conform to a particular religion, we may fall into exclusivism (rejection of other faiths) and inclusivism (acceptance of spiritual power in other faiths, but rejection of their salvation). In the last chapter we discussed the necessity of human nature subscribing to a social order. Within that structure we would survive only with cooperation and such cooperation must have rules. These rules of social cooperation are the basis of religion. While the rules may vary from one religion to another, rules are necessary to keep the hierarchical structure firm.

Usually we experience our dedication to an organized religion with a sense of obligation. Thus we conform to the rules because of the internal pressure of our conscience. If we ever think about questioning the doctrine of our religion, we are ridden with guilt for betraying authority. If we fulfill the laws of authority, we are free from guilt, but often fall into passivity.

Spirituality, on the other hand, doesn't offer any standard set of answers to chosen questions or an obligatory way of life. Nor does spirituality offer us a community in which to share beliefs and behaviors that make us feel at home, confident that we are right. As Beatrice Burteau discovered: "Spirituality is not a comfort, it is a risk."

FROM RELIGION TO SPIRITUALITY

In his enlightenment, the Buddha found that on the road to higher consciousness, we do not need to accept what we hear from authorities or tradition. We need not accept a statement just because it is found in our religion book or because it is in accord with our belief. "Be lamps unto yourselves," he said. Rely upon yourselves and not upon authority and you shall reach the heights. In other words, we cannot become spiritual by listening to others tell us about God. We cannot become spiritual because we follow a particular tradition or organized tradition. Spirituality rests squarely upon our own shoulders. It's an inner work. According to Huston Smith, after the Buddha's enlightenment, people came to him and asked:

"Are you a god?"

"No."

"Are you an angel?"

"No."

"Are you a saint?"

"No."

"Then what are you?"

"I am Awake."

The word *Buddha* means "To wake up and to know." When he reached enlightenment, the Buddha "woke up" to truth. He followed his own path just as Socrates, Moses, Jesus, and Muhammad followed their own paths. The confines of the religions observed by the masses were much too limiting for these great heroes who freed themselves from earthly authority to follow the divine voice within. Not surprisingly each of them was condemned by the religion of their culture.

In the West, Carl G. Jung is a hero to some on their way to spirituality. Jung's father was a pastor in the Lutheran

Reformed Church and his mother was the daughter of a pastor. As a child, he attended many funerals. From his father's funeral sermons, Jung learned that Jesus "took" people to himself. For him, this meant "putting them in a hole in the ground." The funerals plus an extraordinary dream when he was a child left him with the belief that God was a "man-eater." When his mother read to him about the world religions, Jung was fascinated with illustrations of the Hindu deities – Brahma, Vishnu, and Shiva. His interest in comparative religions started with the book his mother read to him and lasted throughout his life.

Jung tells of a startling religious experience he had in his boyhood. He saw God sitting on His golden throne high above the world. From this throne an "enormous turd" fell upon the cathedral shattering it to pieces. The experience not only foreshadowed his dispute with the traditional Christian Church, but it gave him insight into his father's problem. Because his father, a Protestant minister, had followed the church's dogmas to the extreme, he had never personally experienced God's healing grace. Unconsciously, his father had substituted church dogma for a direct relationship with the living God. Eventually his father lost his faith.

Like Socrates, Jung spent his life researching the contents of the soul. He discovered that every human being has an instinct or drive toward spiritual wholeness. Although the spiritual process can be a tortuous and slippery path, he found that this inner drive constantly pushes us toward fulfilling our truest self. The inspiration that led him to realize this inner quest in all human beings came to Jung from reading Richard Wilhelm's translation of the Chinese book, *The Secret of the Golden Flower.*

While reading Chinese philosophy Jung discovered what Leonardo Di Vinci and others had discovered long before, that the cosmos and human beings obey the same law – humans are microcosms of the universal macrocosm. The soul and the cosmos are to each other as the inner world and the outer world. Humans participate in all cosmic events because inwardly and outwardly we are interwoven with them. The Tao (the Way) governs us as it does invisible and visible nature (heaven and earth). As the Tao gives rise to darkness and light -- *yin* and *yang*, we too participate in these seemingly opposing principles. With this Jung realized that our aspiration for the spiritual is the innate urge of life to realize itself consciously.

THE SPIRITUAL QUEST

Spirituality then is a personal quest for truth and reality. It has no presuppositions, no doctrines, no dogmas, and no comfort zone. We become ourselves as we go along, and the becoming process has no boundaries. It continues to be open and unfinished. As we travel the path we may have to forsake many of our familiar beliefs. Thus only the sincere, only those with deep soul passion, dare to take up the spiritual quest. We must have integrity, courage and commitment. And one of the most difficult qualifications is independence. We must go through the experience alone. No one can do it for us. As T.S. Eliot said, "You will not know where you are going until you arrive."

So what do we have to guide us? We have our own spiritual intuition. Socrates called it his "daimon" (divine voice). Jesus told us the "Kingdom of God is within." Some call it the "master within." Others refer to it as our "inner guide." Recall that for Aurobindo "Intuition sees the truth of things by a direct inner contact." Intuition is not a voice we hear with our physical ears. It is rather the "still small voice within," of which the Psalms speak, or according to Blavatsky, the "Voice of the silence." On our spiritual journey we develop a new kind of love to guide us and with it comes a sense of right and wrong, truth and falsehood, real and unreal. The further we go, the keener this sense becomes. It is the sense of the holy, and once we contact it we begin to feel an inner peace that changes our life forever.

Stepping on the spiritual path does not mean we must run to a monastery, sit alone on a mountaintop, wear monk robes, or take a vow of silence. Most of us have to do the most difficult task of all – continue our workaday life. Getting away from the world to concentrate on our spiritual task would be much easier than continuing the everyday grind that involves our job, relationships, pleasures and pain, and economic ups and downs. We must "be *in* the world but not *of* it." Enjoy the world, but not get caught up in the vanities of the world. It is important to stay in touch with our actual experience in spirituality and not drawn into involvement with the ego dualities that make up the materialistic world of finance, fame, and social glitter.

As we go deeper within, we gradually move away from authority into our own mystical and moral experiences. Some of our experiences may change and others may stay the same. Many of our experiences could be identical to those recorded by mystics through the ages. Other of our experiences may change as we delve more deeply into the arts and sciences. Scientists continue to uncover information about nature and her workings. What scientists are discovering today integrates well into what mystics have written about for centuries – that everything in the universe is interrelated.

For many in the East, experience is more important than theology or what a person believes. Most look to anyone they think can help them in their quest to experience higher consciousness and God. They don't care what religion a person professes if that person has had insights, realizations, and contacts with the divine. Most of them are happy to consult any person who has had living touch with the divine – the Absolute Supreme Reality. They do this hoping to be helped to have their own experiences. Based on their view of human nature, Easterners point to different paths for different people. People of devotion are drawn to the path of love. Philosophers and intellectuals may prefer the path of knowledge. Others choose the path of service or the path of mental discipline. These are paths of experience tread by great spiritual seekers for thousands of years. The paths are not theories or speculation or belief systems rather they are methods that guide the seeker away from the ego personality to the divine self.

Jesus the Christ

Like Eastern spirituality, Jesus did not prescribe a set of rules, doctrines, or dogmas. He did not call us to be Christians. Jesus called us to awaken, to change our way, to repent. He told those around him that they would be higher than the angels and that the things he did, they would also do, and greater (John 14: 12). Jesus was aware of himself as a complete human being in total unity with God. "I and the Father are one." And he added, "As I am so can you be." To show us that we are gods in the making, he quoted from the Judaic tradition: "Is it not written in your law, 'I said you are gods'?" (John 10:34).

Christ, actually the Christos, is a state of consciousness. Christ was not Jesus' last name. The Aramaic term for the Greek word "Christ" is M'shekha (Messiah) meaning the ideal form of humanity – the Christos. According to Teilhard de Chardin, the Christos is a transpersonal condition of being that all of us will some day become. Jesus did not say this higher state of consciousness was his alone, and he did not call us to worship him. He called us to *follow* him, to learn from him. Jesus lived a God-centered life and called on us to live a God-centered life. He relied on God's authority, not the authority of a particular religion. He threw the letter of the law to the winds to fulfill the spirit of the law. He suggested that we pray in private yet carry the Christ with us among others. The Kingdom is within us. Divinity is our birthright, our inheritance, nearer to us – say the Sufi mystics – than the jugular vein. Jesus called us to awaken, "to flow back into God." He challenged us to transcend our self-centered ego and move into a higher state of divine consciousness. Lama Govinda phrased it, "a turning about in the deepest seat of consciousness." For Aurobindo it meant waking our heart, mind, and soul to the divine consciousness.

When we step on the spiritual path, we begin to realize that ego-power is the source of all the world's troubles. That is the true meaning of sin. Recall the meaning of sin – to miss the mark. Sin is not merely misbehaving, but the transgression of the divine law or cosmic principle – the failure to be centered in God – to be off target. If the aim of evolution and growth is to awaken us to the divinity, then when we are guilty of sin we are failing to be God-conscious in our behavior and thought. What is the remedy for this sinful world? According to the great mystics, the remedy is for each of us to change our consciousness. God does not condemn us for our sins; we condemn ourselves by our sins. God's presence is always with us as unconditional love when we turn our hearts and minds to God. As Jesus said, the first and the great commandment is to love God with all your heart and soul and mind.

The second commandment is to love your neighbor as yourself. It matters not if our neighbor loves us. The spiritual experience we seek is to love our neighbor. If we always remember that God's love is unconditional, we leap beyond the reach of those who condemn us. We may feel pain from others, but they cannot offend us in spirit. Thus we feel, even more strongly than the pain, an inner peace. Deep in our soul we understand the words, "Turn the other cheek," "Resist not evil," and "Forgive them, they know not what they do" – the sermon that Jesus preached with his life.

As long as people war in their hearts and minds, said Aurobindo, we will have wars in the world. The world can only get better when there are more aware and loving people in it. The Mother continually reminded us: God's unconditional love and grace are always there for the asking. If God were to withdraw love and grace for a second, the world would topple into oblivion. Plato may have been the first to say, "Love makes the world go 'round." Mystics would definitely agree. We as human beings have the potential to change our condition of living in ignorance or sin to recognition of the sacred nature at the heart of all existence. The world is holy. "We can change," said the Dalai Lama. "Our ultimate nature is pure."

Institutional Christian churches teach that Jesus was the *only* son of God, that through the incarnation he took on a human body so he could die on the cross for our sins, and thus save the world. According to Jesuit priest, Fr. John White,

"That is a sad caricature, a pale reflection of the true story. It turns Jesus into a magical fairy-tale hero and Christianity into a degenerate cult of personality." A century ago Ralph Waldo Emerson criticized Christianity for becoming a religion *about* Jesus when it should be a religion *of* Jesus. The religion *about* Jesus puts him in the sky next to God and asks him to be responsible for us. The religion *of* Jesus asks each of us to take personal responsibility for growing into the state of Christ consciousness that Jesus demonstrated. The religion *about* Jesus tells us that by his death and resurrection, Jesus saved us from original sin. But Jesus did not save people, he *freed* them from the bondage of the ego. The whole idea is not that Jesus was human like us, but that we have the potential to be gods like him. Fr. White believes that the Christian tradition, rightly understood, seeks to have us all become as Jesus – one in Christ. Recall again John 10:34: "Is it not written in your law, 'I said, you are gods'?"

According to all spiritual teachers, each of us has the God-given right to enter the divine realm, to be healed of our sense of separation and alienation – to transcend ignorance and the fear of death. There is no exclusion of certain races, gender, profession, thieves, politicians, or anyone. These spiritual teachers include all people willing to grow beyond the ego and become holy and pure. They show us the way to a higher state of being and call upon us to realize it, to make it real, and to actualize it in our everyday lives.

Throughout history spiritual teachers have shown us the way to the Kingdom of God, but they did not, nor could they take anyone there – not by rapture, space ships, or group suicide – because the Kingdom of God is not a place, it is a state of consciousness. We discover also that heaven and hell are not places, but states of consciousness. Heaven is union with God and hell is separation from God. We cannot measure heaven and hell in terms of miles but in the condition of our soul. As with the Buddha, entering the Kingdom or Heaven or Nirvana depends on our own effort – our willingness to let go of our ego (our personal desires) and surrender to the highest within us.

A New Set of Lenses

Western religions that guarantee salvation if you believe in their founder and idolize their scripture, left thinking people unfulfilled. For example, that Jesus died for our sins and we are to worship him as the *only* Son of God or wind up in the fires of torment seemed unfair to other faiths. Religions *about* Jesus place heaven and hell in outer space. In one sermon a preacher said if a rocket ship could go straight up an unlimited distance, it would land in heaven. These religions concentrate on the external – places in space, a book, and the historical person of Jesus. Sadly lacking is any awareness of inner space – of involving consciousness and evolving consciousness. As people grew in awareness, many of them drifted away from exoteric religion of the masses to follow an inner path that leads to the truth preserved in its esoteric tradition.

Some people scorn the practice of *yoga* saying it is not Christian. However, Matthew 11: 29-30 suggests that Jesus taught his disciples to "take my yoke upon you...my yoke is easy." The word "yoke" comes from the Sanskrit *yug*, meaning "to yoke or join." Thus "yoke" has the same root as the word "yoga." Yoga is a system of spiritual practices designed to unite our lower ego nature to our higher spiritual nature, thereby attaining union with the divine. Yoking with God is exactly what Jesus taught, not that there would always be an unbridgeable gulf between God and us.

Through rote words, blind faith, and mechanical behavior, we could never experience unity with the divine. We could only follow the rules based on authoritarian doctrines and rituals of institutional religions. However, for some of us such procedures are no longer satisfactory. We are not simply "yea sayers," we are becoming more aware of our ability to take conscious control of our evolution and look within for our answers.

Spiritual teachers have always taught that human destiny is to grow to a higher state of being and ultimately return to the Godhead, which is our true self. Krishna, Buddha, Lao Tzu, Moses, Zoroaster, Muhammad, Mahavira, Quetzalcoatl,

Guru Nanak and others came with the message to let go of our slavery to the ego-ignorance, to our personal desires and selfishness, and unite with the highest that is within us. Krishna called it Atman, the Buddha called it Nirvana, Lao Tzu spoke of the Tao, and Zoroaster of Ahura Mazda. But the names were merely the language of their culture meaning the Supreme Reality. The message of these spiritual teachers and sages and saviors transcends any sect or religion. If these enlightened individuals were to meet, I doubt there would be any argument among them, only agreement. Unfortunately, the unenlightened – the masses bathed in ego – argue about what is or is not true.

The way to God-realization is through an ascent in consciousness to knowledge and unconditional love for all creation. If we continue to stay in the ego-consciousness, don't be surprised if we continue to have wars and global catastrophes. Is each of us part of the problem? Look in the mirror. In us lies the answer. Do we see ego in the mirror, or do we through a new set of lenses, see Atman, Christ, or the Buddha Nature in the heart of our being? It is up to us to work out our own salvation by steadfastly following the spiritual path. Pop answers and quick fixes would be nice, but they won't help. What will help? According to those who have climbed the spiritual ladder: to renew our minds and hearts by awakening to the presence of the divinity in us, in others, and in everything in the world.

Chapter Eleven

How Free Are We?

What do you suppose will satisfy the soul,
except to walk free and own no superior?

Walt Whitman

Fate or Freewill?

*T*he question of freewill or fate is the most knotty of all metaphysical questions and nobody has been able to solve it to everyone's satisfaction. Students of karma and re-birth believe that we choose our parents, our gender, our nation, our race, our environment, and perhaps even the shape of our nose. Unfortunately, in our ignorant state, these choices are "unconscious" to our waking state, and therefore, not "free" in the sense that we are aware of having made them. There is a deep level in the soul that Hindus call *Purusha* (the witness) that knows and directs what we need to experience in the present life to give us the necessary lessons to learn for spiritual growth. The kind of life Purusha selects will depend upon our past attitudes and interests, thoughts, and actions.

Most students of reincarnation and karma believe that the law of karma contains both our fate and our freedom. In the West, we call the law of karma "justice," thus fate is all that we bring to this life from the past, and freedom is the attitude we use to deal with what we get. Attitude is the most important factor in our lives: *what* we are facing now is dependent upon our past attitudes, and the future depends on *how* we face events in our lives now. It is never too late to change our attitude. If we rebel against life's problems and blame others for our unhappiness, in all probability we will suffer the consequences. We may feel stress, anxiety, guilt, and anger. On the other hand, if we face life's ordeals by asking ourselves what we can learn from our suffering and joy, and treat others with loving kindness, we also reap the results.

Up to this point in human evolution, the world of the five senses has been our safe and familiar environment, and some philosophers and scientists have set this physical world of sensation as the boundaries of human experience. But other philosophers, mystics, saints, and seers have experienced a world beyond the physical, a vast and beautiful spiritual realm that most of us have only caught glimpses of through the arts and sciences. We know the mind is more complex than the emotions: it has the ability to conceptualize, analyze, and reflect – yet it too can lead us into false reasoning and self-delusion. The power of our thoughts can be a force for health, growth, and change or we can fall into unhealthy habit patterns that affect our health adversely.

The reasoning mind is the instrument that integrates and interprets the stream of sensory data that bombards us from everywhere. But the reason can be colored by emotion, just as emotions can be conditioned by our thoughts. So how free are we? Certainly much of our freedom lies in realizing that once we understand that we are the cause of our happiness and unhappiness, we stop blaming the world and other people and start cooperating with the divine law. Some people compare freedom to learning the game: if I try to cheat God's law or universal justice, I cheat myself. Feeling revengeful gets me nowhere. When Mahatma Gandhi's friends wanted to seek revenge against the British, Gandhi shook his head sadly: "An eye for an eye making the whole world blind." Taking revenge is easy, but forgiveness requires courage of the mind and the emotions. When we learn to forgive ourselves, we find it easier to forgive others, and forgiving ourselves is a never-ending process. Recall when Peter asked Jesus, "When my brother wrongs me, how often must I forgive him? Seven times?" "No," Jesus replied, "not seven times; I say, seventy times seven times" (Matt. 18: 21-22).

Forgiveness

When we have touched another with forgiveness we no longer require anything in return. Forgiveness is a letting go of unresolved issues such as feelings of being betrayed by the body, by friends, and by the world. Forgiveness is letting go of our identification with such states as fear, resentment, and guilt. It presents the possibility of freedom from the ancient incarcerations of the judging mind. Perhaps the best teachers of forgiveness are dogs. If we are late, we receive a tongue licking, not a tongue-lashing. Even when we scold them, they want to be with us. They are totally forgiving. Cats are forgiving, too, but they make us work for it.

At first forgiveness feels awkward, because we often must forgive in another the qualities we have long judged in ourselves. We may be opening our minds and hearts to another, but forgiving is primarily a means of self-healing. Cancer patients often practice healing by sending forgiveness into their tumors, their immune system, and their whole being. Forgiveness flows through the being with healing energy. The physical body may not suddenly leap up and shout, "I'm healthy again" – but one is healthy again in their soul. Forgiveness presents the possibility of freedom from the judging mind. It allows anger to float in a merciful awareness and allows the mind to flow beyond the sense of separation. Practiced daily, forgiveness opens the mind to the natural compassion of the heart.

Moral Choices

Real forgiveness takes an understanding of the spiritual law, for we are only as free as we are knowledgeable of the divinity. Because most people are not very knowledgeable in this respect, we continue to disagree on what is right and what is wrong. For two thousand years we in the West have been taught that God gave us freewill to choose between good and evil. However, individuals and religions disagree on what is good and what is evil. Morality is a dilemma. If God gave us freewill to make choices, why do we make wrong choices, when at the time we make the choices, we believe they are right? St. Paul experienced the identical problem: "I cannot even understand my own actions. I do not do what I want to do but what I hate... What happens is that I do, not the good I will to do, but the evil I do not intend..." (Romans 7:15, 19). None of us purposefully makes wrong choices. If we purposely make wrong choices it would be saying, "I know this food is poison, but I'll eat it anyway." If we realize the food is poisoned we won't eat it. Unless we have mental problems, we never intentionally wish to harm the body. Would any of us intentionally choose an act that was poison to the soul?

Socrates, who is considered the father of moral philosophy, had some insights on the subject of freedom. He said if we truly "know" that an act is immoral, we would not do it. "Know" is the key word here. For Socrates, to "know" means to *Know Thyself,* and that is freedom. We call this intuitive type of knowing *archetypal knowledge,* which is different from knowing how to ride a bicycle, to play Trivial Pursuit, or to argue a case in court. For Socrates, knowledge of the self belongs to the spiritually virtuous person who realizes the highest goal in life is to "make the soul as good as possible." Socrates taught that goodness and knowledge always go together. To have knowledge of scripture without practicing its teachings in everyday life is no more real knowledge than is being a good person in everyday life without understanding the principle of the archetypal Good. He believed that only the person who knows what the highest good of the soul is and practices that knowledge regularly reaches the freedom of self-mastery.

The spiritually wise person doesn't rely on social approval or other human authority. Could you imagine Jesus turning to Caesar or even a Sadducee for advice? Could you imagine the Buddha asking the Mafia how to raise money for travel expenses? Could you imagine Muhammad seeking advice from idol worshippers? Or Moses telling his people in the wilderness, "I quit!" In these highly virtuous and intuitive souls dwelled spiritual knowledge. Nothing tempted them away from the truth. If now and then we turn away from truth it is because we have yet to reach spiritual knowledge.

Socrates said if we have true knowledge of what is best for our soul we will always choose to do it. He thought we would never freely turn against such knowledge to commit an evil act. That would be like choosing to drive on the wrong side of the freeway in heavy traffic. We know the only way to avoid accidents is to drive on the right side of the freeway. Driving on the wrong side means we have either had too much to drink or need psychological help.

Usually, said Socrates, we commit evil acts expecting some personal gain. The thief would rather steal a stereo than get a job. The thief might agree that stealing is wrong, but in his ignorance of the spiritual law, he believes stealing outweighs working, thus he benefits from stealing. Rebirth philosophers believe that in some lifetime the thief will aspire toward genuine knowledge and realize the act of stealing poisons the soul. With that realization, the stealing ends. We may think that the thief's progress is too slow until we remember the Hindu claim: "God is not in a hurry."

Jesus agreed with Socrates when he said, "If you *know* what you are doing, you are blessed. If you *do not know*, you are cursed." Acting in knowledge involves truth, whereas acting in ignorance entails falsehood. When we overindulge in food, sex, or drugs, anger, envy, criticizing others, reading trash or gossip, we are acting in ignorance and are thus unaware of any damage to the soul.

Let's image that a brilliant businessman named Edward Carpenter accumulates wealth at the expense of others. To avoid opposition Ed forces potential competitors into bankruptcy. "That's the way the game is played," says Ed. "Good guys finish last, and I'm a winner." His acts may be unethical, but he is the first to point out they are not illegal. Socrates might ask Ed, "Is the exploitation of your soul worth it?" But Ed doesn't care about souls. He wants to achieve recognition and respect from others for his worldly success. In fact the community considers Ed an outstanding citizen and asks him to run for political office. Ed is a winner.

Ed has accomplished what he set out to accomplish, but he is still dissatisfied. No matter how much pleasure we get from wealth and recognition, unless we live for the good of the soul our lives lack peace. Ed's soul is dis/eased (ill-at-ease) because he is a prisoner of ignorance and ego. According to students of reincarnation, Ed could return as a person subjected to other unscrupulous competitors or something similar. Ed is not an evil person. He doesn't torture animals, maim children, or batter his wife – he is merely ignorant of the good of his soul and how his unawareness has harmed others.

Resist Not Evil

With the law of universal justice in mind, let's take a look at our own condition. When an individual or group unfairly accuses and taunts us, ought we to ask ourselves "Is this a lesson I need to learn?" Socrates said it is better to receive an injustice than to cause an injustice to another. And he knew of what he spoke: The Athenians demanded Socrates' death because he dared to be different. The Buddha clearly stated the results of indignation: "He reviled me, he beat me, then plundered me, [those] who express such thoughts tie their mind with the intention of retaliation. In them hatred will not cease...in the minds of those who do not think like this, hatred *will* cease" (*Dhammapada*. Twin verses: 3,4). "Hatred," explained the Buddha, "does not cease by hatred...hatred ceases by love." Jesus agreed. He taught that to reach our spiritual self we must love our neighbor and forgive our enemy.

Both Buddha and Jesus taught that the awful dark anger that a transgressor arouses in us gives power to evil forces. They said to "resist not evil," because the more we fight against these dark forces, the more bitter we become and bitterness causes deep scars in our soul. Jung observed that angry reactions were projections of our own negativity onto others. When the projection hooks onto the other person, there are then two angry people rather than just one. However, if we learn to forgive the other person for their transgressions, both parties will be better off. The difficult part is – the forgiveness must be sincere. Patting ourselves on the back for forgiving is an ego trip. The minute I think, "I am superior for not reacting to your addle-headed anger," I've fallen flat on my face.

Discipline

Forgiveness takes discipline, but freedom is tied to discipline. When I lose my temper and react in anger, am I really free to respond with ability, or am I a puppet of my anger? Discipline takes courage and perseverance, but it pays off. Athletes that discipline their body perform in ways the average person cannot. If we discipline our mind, we are freer to explore the world of ideas than other people. If we discipline our emotions, then our responses are under control. Mystics of every tradition have said the highest human freedom is spiritual knowledge. Such knowledge includes discipline of the body, the emotions, and the mind, thus allowing the spiritual light to shine through.

Recall the sun analogy: each cloud, from envy to pride, is a cloud of ego obscuring the sun of spiritual freedom. Brushing the clouds away is no easy task, but as long as they befog our lives, our will is tied to ignorance. Freedom is a responsibility that calls for discipline. When we search deeply, we realize that we are only as free as we are conscious of the divinity in our lives.

Interpretation of Scripture

Upon reaching higher consciousness we will understand the meaning of life and the universe. At the present stage in evolution most people argue the meaning of spiritual knowledge as well as the universe. Take the Ten Commandments that Yahweh gave to Moses on Mt. Sinai nearly three thousand years ago. The commandment "Thou shalt not kill" sounds simple enough and most people agree that this is a good commandment – killing is wrong. But if another country declares war on us, killing the enemy becomes a patriotic duty. With the exception of the conscientious objector, no one believes that killing the enemy in defense of the country is wrong. Does that mean killing in some cases is right? Does the Commandment say that? Or does the Commandment mean that killing is wrong only if it involves taking a life in cold-blooded murder? Does the Commandment say that? Is the Commandment referring to killing on the physical level alone, or does it include the mental and emotional levels as well? Hateful and sarcastic statements can instantly kill a creative thought or a feeling of warmth.

The Bible says human beings have dominion over animals, but where does it say we have a right to kill animals by torturing them in the laboratories to test tobacco, army weapons, cancer or psychological pain? Yahweh said, "See, I give you every seed-bearing plant all over the earth and every tree that has seed-bearing fruit on it to be your food" (Gen. 1: 20). Where does Yahweh say it is all right to kill animals for sport, or even eat them? Those who look to the Bible as their authority might say, "Oh, stop nit-picking, you know what the Commandment means." But do we?

If individuals and religious organizations disagree on the meaning of even one Commandment, are we likely to disagree on the meaning of others? The Commandment, "Thou shalt not steal," is a pronouncement of our duty to Yahweh, to ourselves, and to others to abstain from taking what does not belong to us. We all know and appreciate that, but do we really, deeply, know it? Would we steal if we were starving or our children or our pets? Are such exceptions allowed? Do you know anyone who brings pencils, paper, or floppy discs home from the office – or scotch tape at Christmas to seal packages? Parents teach their children not to steal, then return home from vacation with a hotel towel, stationary, or soap. "They expect you to take them," is the off-the-cuff answer. Then why sneak them out? Have you ever been in a picnic area where you found a fishing pole, knife, or camera the previous picnickers left on the table? What a trustworthy world this would be if the previous picnickers could drive back to the picnic area and find what they left behind. Can our soul be free when we take small hotel items or equipment left behind?

People frequently turn to religious authorities for answers to questions about good and evil and the meaning of the Ten Commandments. But religious authorities are often caught in the dogma of their particular denomination, thus they disagree with each other. Quakers believe it is always wrong to kill another human being – war or no war. Mormons believe if the president of our country declares war it is their duty to fight. Baptists are opposed to drinking alcoholic beverages. Catholics use wine in the Holy Eucharist and drink alcohol on social occasions. Anglicans and Nazarenes disagree whether Jesus at the Cana wedding changed water into wine or into grape juice.

Fundamental religious authorities believe our lives should be centered in the family unit. Men and women are duty-bound to marry, and the wife's place is in the home with her husband as spiritual mentor. Liberal religious authorities agree that the family as a loving unit is good, but what happens to the single person who prefers a career, or to gays and lesbians who are innately unsuited for heterosexual marriage? Do these institutions actually base their teachings on scripture or upon their interpretation of scripture?

Unfinished Products

Aurobindo and the Mother believed that we each try to do what is best according to our individual level of consciousness, but until we reach enlightenment of the divinity within, we are bound to think and to act in some degree of ignorance. So often we build prison bars around our consciousness. The religious man who insists that men are spiritually superior to women may be projecting his own fear of women and therefore need to get in touch with the feminine aspect of his soul. He may be afraid to question his identity. And the woman afraid to face the responsibility of individual equality may project the masculine aspect of her soul on men. Afraid to question her own self-identity, she fights to carry on the subservient feminine role. But true femininity as true masculinity is a soul quality. To be our true selves, we must look beyond the physical. Men can cut a business deal and still have poetry in their soul. Women can lovingly nurture and still make logical decisions.

Aurobindo agreed with Teilhard de Chardin that our souls are unfinished products in the evolutionary journey. In that case we are all trying to rise above Aristotle's definition of the human being: "Man is a rational animal." Basically we are striving for perfection, or according to Jung, who was uncomfortable with the term *perfection*, we are striving toward *wholeness*. The journey, he said, is arduous as we weave the tapestry of our lives through joy and sorrow, fortune and misfortune. But the closer we get to the "Holy Grail," the freer we become.

Looking back in history, we see more clearly the progress we have made. We no longer throw Christians to the lions or burn heretics at the stake, but when we think of the 3,000,000 Jews gassed in concentration camps by the Nazis and all those who turned their heads without lifting a finger to help, we may wonder how far the progress has really come. Yet, we do see progress in the new consciousness arising in our concern for the environment, caring for the planet, animal rights, civil rights, and in individuals involved in conscious spiritual growth. These concerns are slowly filtering into the mass consciousness.

Aurobindo considered the *good* everything that moves us closer to the spiritual truth and *evil* all the obstacles we put in our way. Gandhi said he had never found evil in another person that was not in him. Jesus reinforced it when he admonished us to remove the beam in our own eye before trying to remove the beam in another person's eye. Was Gandhi right? Could we possibly recognize evil in another if it were not in ourselves?

Let's imagine that the term *light* represents *good* and the word *shadow* signifies *evil*. Shadow depends upon light for its existence. Light does not depend upon shadow. Thus evil has no absolute power of self-existence and is only the shadow of good. Evil could not exist without ego or ignorance and ignorance is the shadow of spiritual knowledge and freedom. The shadow of love is hate and the shadow of truth is falsehood. At this stage in our evolution, we are a mixture of these dualities, but as we grow spiritually the light becomes brighter than the shadow, and truth becomes stronger than falsehood.

Perhaps freewill and goodwill are synonymous terms. When we know goodness, we are free of evil tendencies. Goodwill is that which treats all creatures as ends in themselves and never as means only. Albert Schweitzer refused to draw a line between higher forms of life and lower forms. He questioned who of us can truly judge what value other forms of life have in their sharing of the universe. Schweitzer believed all life is precious and he considered it wrong to take any life unnecessarily. "Do we have to pick the flower?" he asked. "Can't we allow it to live?"

Freedom

Personal imperfections frighten us. Due to them we make mistakes, get discouraged, feel guilt, fall ill, grow old and die. So often we look in the wrong places for happiness. It seems as difficult for us to see life in its totality as it is for a thirteen-year-old in love to project the future. Our attention is fixed only on the present moment in time and in direct relationship to ourselves rather than seeing our relationship to everything in the universe. And this is the difference between the imprisoning ego and freedom.

Due to our limited knowledge of our real self, we experience both physical and psychological pain. Some disciplined yogis have the ability to control physical pain. Others of us take an aspirin. Indian saint Ramakrishna grappled with an extreme case of throat cancer. Once when the doctor probed his throat, Ramakrishna winced in pain and the doctor stopped. Ramakrishna said to the doctor, "Wait just a minute." Then he uttered, "All right, go ahead." Ramakrishna placed himself in a state of mind in which the physical pain did not break through into awareness – or barely so.

Psychological pain is as devastating as physical pain, perhaps more so. While physical pain involves nerve sensations, psychological pain thwarts the ego. We want to win a golf tournament, but don't. We want to make money on a deal, but lose. We want to be promoted, but aren't. We want to be invited, but are snubbed. Psychological pain is the pain of pride, which arises by separating ourselves from God.

Jesus said, "Inasmuch as you have done it unto the least of these, you have done it unto me." Humility is the heart of the message. Psychological discipline is the ability to feel the joy of the victor as if it were our own victory. Actually, the victory of another is our victory also. Each of us is a part of the whole and each component has its part to play. Our neighbor's role in the world is as important as our role, and ours is as important as the most famous person in the world. The small role is as necessary in making up the whole as is the large role. In our own body the brain stem is not as noticeable as the hand, but life would cease without it.

Freedom approaches as we begin to understand the necessity of each part of the whole and to rely on intuition for direct insight into truth. We gain freedom when we know our spiritual self and develop unconditional love. We are already the perfection or wholeness we look for outside ourselves, but to understand this, we must grow from ignorance into knowledge – from ego into freedom. The journey is well worth the effort because each conscious step brings us closer to freeing the divine presence within.

Chapter Twelve

After Death –
Then What?

I am making my last effort to return to
that which is divine in me to that which
is divine in the universe.

The last words of Plotinus

Near Death Experience

*T*hanks to the pioneering efforts of Dr. Elizabeth Kubler-Ross and Dr. Richard Moody, Western society has begun to look at death in a new light. Many of their patients and other patients have given personal reports about near-death/out-of-body experiences. The common thread running through all the reports is that death is not something to fear.

Although no two people have exactly the same experience, just as no two people experience music or mathematics in exactly the same way, a common pattern in these NDE (Near-Death-Experiences) appears. They report a feeling of peace and well being without bodily sensations or fear. They view the body from a point somewhere above it. Their sense of sight and/or hearing is heightened. They are very alert and their consciousness is clear. Many are aware of moving rapidly through a dark tunnel toward a light. When they reach the light, they report meeting a luminous being of such great love that they call it Christ or if in another culture, the Buddha or Muhammad. With this being they communicate telepathically and find themselves in a beautifully blissful state. Some meet dead relatives and friends and talk to them. They are often told to return to the body, that their work is not finished on earth. Most people report that they return to the body reluctantly. Upon their return, their lives seem transformed.

Their attitudes toward life and death change. They become interested in leading a spiritual life and have no fear of dying.

Spence Wallace, an adult college student, gave the following report of his NDE. The accident he describes left him a paraplegic. He wrote:

> My friend and I were traveling westbound on the Interstate in his new roadster. As we crossed the overpass in Portland, Oregon the car skidded on a sheet of ice and spun out of control. I was thrown from the car 255 feet out and 85 feet down, where I landed on my back across a railroad track. In an instant, I was separated from the physical world as I knew it.
>
> My out-of-body experience began as I felt as if I was up above the accident scene and I could see it all. It was dark outside, yet the whole area was illuminated with white and blue light. I could see my body lying on the rail all twisted and bloody. It was not moving. I could see the details of the area surrounding me clearly. There was broken glass, rocks, weeds browned by winter, and windblown paper caught by the taller weeds and bushes. It was like viewing everything from a wide-angle camera lens, and the lens opened to show more of the scene.
>
> I could see the car upside down in the weeds about 175 feet away from my body, with steam escaping from the engine compartment. A tire on the car was spinning slowly around and around. I could not see my friend anywhere, so I reasoned that he must be under the car. My wide-angle lens expanded again, and I could see the freeway and overpass with the cars and trucks zipping

along. Something was missing. I could not hear the sounds of traffic, nor could I hear the ringing in my ears that I've grown accustomed to hearing because of a punctured eardrum when I was eight years old.

Every sense that is within the human body is absent within the spirit. It was freezing cold outside, yet I was not cold. I felt no pain, nor any sensations that occurred in the physical world. I was experiencing a peace that I had never known before, a peace that words could not describe. It was a feeling of security and tranquility, and what had happened below was unimportant. I felt no emotion while watching my physical body die. The last thing I can recall was that I was being pulled through space with that same white and blue light – and I remember nothing else.

I had multiple injuries. My left femur was shattered and three of my vertebra. My ribs had pushed through vital organs throughout my chest and abdominal cavity. Breathing was difficult because I was drowning in my own blood. When the paramedics reached me, my blood pressure was forty over ten and I was going into shock. Some time during the eight hours of surgery, my heart stopped beating, but they brought me back. For the next sixteen days, I lived totally off life-support machines. I was in a coma, and it was iffy that I would pull through.

As to be expected my philosophy regarding life has changed dramatically. I feel that what I experienced was more positive than negative, and I feel that it has made me a better person. I no longer take anything for granted and can see the good in every bad or unpleasant experience. Good cannot be appreciated unless one experiences some bad. My attitudes concerning God and my fellow man have changed, too, and I am much more comfortable in dealing with both. Above all I now realize that life here on earth is nothing more than a series of events, some good and some bad. Whatever events happen, they cannot be changed. What matters, is how we deal with them. A positive outlook will always make things bearable, no matter what the situation. Finally, I have discovered that life is a learning process and I make the majority of decisions. I may not always make the right decision, and when I don't, I know that I can live with it.

I still don't know all the answers to the questions I have thought about, and I doubt very much that I will as long as I am here in the world. If I have anything to say about death and dying, I would say that death should not be feared. It is a transformation into a world that has no boundaries or limits. It is life without the laws of physics or science, and it is the purest form of living.

The last time Spence and I talked he said he was going to build a cabin in the north woods. I studied my paraplegic student sitting in his wheel chair. "How will you put the roof on?" He grinned. "I've invented some pulleys..."

Physical Death

Children ask why people and pets have to die. Adults often skirt the subject. How many times have we heard someone say, "Let's talk about something else – death is so morbid"? This is one side of our dual nature, but the other side of us is fascinated with death. The highest rated TV shows are filled with violence and death. Yet, when a family member or friend contracts a fatal disease, we carefully avoid the subject

of death. Why? Because TV shows do not involve us emotionally. We are not touched by personal loss. Family and friends
on the other hand affect us deeply. Through them, we come
face to face with our own mortality. We are so used to identifying family and friends by their physical body that we
sometimes forget that human beings are much more than
flesh that grows old, catches colds, struggles with diabetes,
arthritis, or cancer. When the physical body dies we speak as
if it were the whole person: "Poor Jud is dead." Certainly the
life force as we know it has left Jud's body, but is Jud only his
body? Theosophists remind us that we are "spiritual beings
standing among material things." The body is merely the most
physical component of our entire make-up.

Time/Space

Plato described human beings as the bridge between the dualism of the material universe and the highest spiritual unity.
We are finite and infinite, both flawed and good, both mortal
and immortal, both darkness and light. We are a combination
of matter and spirit. The divine essence in us is immortal and
cannot die. The soul of each individual is growing toward its
immortality.

When we speak of birth and death, we are positing the
necessity of time/space for the soul's journey. According to
philosophers of consciousness evolution, the soul needs to
experience *time* on a finite basis. In time our soul travels
through successive lives to accumulate knowledge of the divinity. Aurobindo said the soul holds all of life's experiences
in its subconscious and superconscious memory, thus death
becomes a necessity because the only means finite life and
mind have to attain immortality is with a living physical
body.

As we progress to higher states of consciousness, bodily
forms change to better serve the needs of the soul.
Anthropologists have found that the human body today is
more refined than it was millions of years ago. To the extent
the soul evolves, the body must also evolve to work as a ser-
viceable instrument. I doubt that the mind of an Einstein

could have functioned through the brain structure of a homo-
sapien thirty thousand years ago. Nor could our minds.

Fear of Death

Our fear of death is deeply rooted in our fear of being de-
voured, broken up, and destroyed. We fear the loss of our
senses, our thoughts, our will, and our feelings. We fear the
awful finality that death suggests – the end of our aspirations,
and the breaking off from family, friends, and personal interests. Even if we believe in personal salvation after death, we
cannot wholly abolish the fear of death's sting, so we try to
deny death by pushing thoughts of it aside.

Viewing the process of life and death as two sides of the
same coin offers little comfort. We perceive them as opposites
in the same way we think of the world filled with objects
separated from each other, rather than viewing the connecting link in all things. Existential philosopher Soren Kierkegaard
believed our separation from God makes us anxious, nervous, guilt-ridden, depressed, and afraid of the world and of
each other. He called our existential predicament the fall from
our original and essential relationship with God into an existence separated from God.

The Fall and the Return

Viewed metaphorically, Adam and Eve's fall from the Garden
of Paradise could be the story of humanity's need to journey
from an unconsciousness state to total consciousness. Adam
and Eve, the prototypes of humankind, lived with God in
Paradise. They could not realize their state of bliss any more
than an unborn baby can realize its condition of safety in the
womb. "The Fall" would be the necessary birth of the soul
from the womb of unconscious bliss into the experience of
matter, life, and mind – the necessary conditions for human
growth.

What would we learn by living in a state of bliss unconsciously? For God to tell Adam and Eve not to eat of the Tree
of Knowledge or they will be punished would be like telling

a hungry six-month-old baby not to cry or she will be spanked. Freewill can only be utilized by conscious and responsible beings, not by an unconscious Adam and Eve who had absolutely no understanding of obedience or disobedience. Once the reasoning process develops, freewill comes into play for making choices. Kierkegaard said that through reason we experience separation from God because the rational mind identifies with the dual world. As we progress, souls surely will burst free from the limitations of separation into the freedom of uniting with the Divinity. At that point we will experience the Garden of Paradise fully conscious. When we realize our true spirituality in unconditional love, our present way of thinking that we are broken up and destroyed by death may give way to love's immortality.

Rebirth gives the soul its opportunity to grow step-by-step, life-by-life, into wholeness or human perfection. As it climbs spiritually, won't the soul need physical bodies with greater spiritual capacity than they now have? Students of rebirth believe that until we form the flawless "resurrected body" the body of each life will be discarded and a new body formed for the soul's next experience. Aurobindo suggested that the soul could not progress without a physical body for its dwelling place, because at this stage of our evolution we are children of this planet. He found that the best way to make the physical world ready for the divinity on earth is through progress of our soul while in physical bodies. Thus death becomes necessary, not as a denial of life, but as a process of life as the soul aspires to immortality. If the design of evolution is to spiritualize matter, then consciousness is the key.

Actually there can be no death, if we mean by death, dying into nothing. What we call death is a change of form. The burning log is reduced to ashes, and though it changes form, no energy is lost. If a thousand acres of forest burns to ashes, there is a definite change of form, yet the amount of material energy remains constant. Our human body may die to its life in the world, but according to Einstein's theorem $E = Mc2$, like the log and forest, the material energy of the physical body isn't lost – it merely changes form. If it is true that matter is spirit slowed down – identical in kind, but not in degree – then the process we call death means that matter changes from a familiar energy structure into an unfamiliar one. And because we cannot perceive spiritual energy with our physical eyes as we can the physical body, we fear death, even deny it.

WHAT HAPPENS AFTER WE DIE?

What happens after we die? According to Eastern and Western mystics and investigators of NDE's, the physical body itself appears to have no conscious memory, but the soul is conscious and sees the whole of its past life being presented like a panorama. The soul reads its life as a spectator looking down at the world stage it is leaving with a true understanding of the karmic justice in all the suffering and the happiness it has experienced.

First Stage After Death

Most traditions agree that for a while after death the soul lingers in the earth realm near the body, near the scene of death, or near people and places where there is a strong attachment. It is possible for the soul to communicate with the living for a brief period at the time of death and shortly thereafter. Like many, I was the recipient of that communication:

> During the last stages of my father's cancer, I purchased a new home on the golf course. An avid golfer, my father deeply wanted to see my new home. Since my father was bed-ridden and more than 500 miles away, I took photographs of the new house to him. Two weeks later, about 9:00 Monday morning, I was at the new house watering trees and planting flowers when unexpectedly I felt my father's presence. I could not see his face clearly, but I knew he was smiling and full of joy. For the three hours I worked outside I felt

his presence with me. It was wonderful. Later that afternoon when I arrived home at my old house, a message was on the phone recorder from my mother saying my father had passed away at 8:30 A.M. that morning.

I left immediately to be with my mother. While there, three of my father's friends reported that his "spirit" came to them as if to say goodbye. My sister was the executrix of the estate. She had not felt his presence until one day when she had to make a difficult financial decision. After she made it, she asked, "Dad, did I make the right decision?" He appeared before her nodding his head pleasantly. She said she had never felt so relieved in her life.

How long the soul remains in the earth realm may depend on the soul's development and its particular needs. The process differs among individuals. Dr. Richard Moody found that an earthbound soul hovers close to the dead physical body or scene of death for as long as possible, and if it has a strong identification with the physical realm, it may not realize that it is no longer connected to the physical body. An earth-bound soul is one that during life depended upon a person, money, house, car, or profession for its self-identification – or was attached to addictive habits such as alcohol or drugs. When the soul's energies, including the desires, the senses, and the mind, are poured out into the material world, the soul tends to identify exclusively with the physical body. Everything it knows, loves, and desires binds it to the earth. Its god, so to speak, is physical. For Plato, the earthbound soul is the *irrational* part of the soul – mainly sensuous appetites.

Dr. Moody also discovered that after death the soul (its irrational part) of an alcoholic or heavy drug user inhabits bars and nightclubs where alcohol flows abundantly. A drug user's soul will hover near drug scenes. But the soul of the dead person is frustrated, because it can't taste the alcohol or feel the effect of drugs. This is what some call *hell*. The more earthbound a soul is, the longer it remains frustrated in the subtle physical realm. People alive on earth may not see the deceased, nor do they recognize its subtle physical presence except in some instances when ghosts make themselves felt. Also, these earthbound souls may reincarnate more quickly than other souls. Their desires lure them back quickly to the material world. This cycle continues life after life until the soul at last realizes that there must be something more satisfying than material things.

Gradually, again depending upon the soul's development (According to the *Tibetan Book of the Dead*, some advanced souls may pass immediately through the lower earth and desire planes), the soul's earthbound elements will dissolve slowly or quickly into the physical plane. Most traditions believe that the more advanced the soul the more rapidly the earthbound elements dissolve.

Second Stage After Death

Following the physical plane, the soul enters the vital or desire realm to undergo penance for its offenses. Dr. Kubler-Ross discovered that in all the reports from people who related their near-death-experiences, judgment was not made upon their lives by God, but by the deceased persons themselves. We are our own judges. The whole of the past life flashes in front of the deceased, and at that moment the soul knows its transgressions and omissions and judges itself for what it has done that it should not have done and what it has failed to do. The highly developed soul will learn from this lesson and not perform such transgressions and omissions in its next life. The less highly developed soul would need to experience lesson after lesson until the light dawns.

According to the *Tibetan Book of the Dead*, there are many levels in the after-death desire realm. How long a soul chooses to stay will depend upon the strength of its desires and passions. Ego emotions such as jealousy and envy, resentment and anger will prolong the sojourn if we cling to them after death. Love, sincerity, empathy, and kindness will speed the journey from the desire realm to the mental stage. In the desire realm, we live out again the emotions experienced during our time here on earth. Some souls are strongly attached to ego emotions whereas more spiritually conscious souls allow them to drop away.

Researchers and Shamans have studied the results of suicidal death and report that suicides remain in the desire realm until their life on earth would have normally ended. They claim that the after death state of a suicide is similar to having a nightmare. Whereas you and I wake up from our nightmares and are immediately back into our physical body, suicides have no physical body to return to. Rather than escaping the problems they had on earth, they must experience the nightmare for the rest of their normal life span. When suicides reincarnate, they may have to experience the same or similar problems they faced in the previous life until they courageously face the lessons they must learn.

Many sages and saints have said that we never give ourselves more than we can handle in a lifetime, but our life experiences sometimes seem so overwhelming that we choose to escape through suicide, insanity, drugs, alcohol, food, or a hundred other avenues. Most of us have experienced emotional states similar to the suicide, the addict, the insane, and that is why we are able to identify with them. Even in our present life some of us have considered suicide, but for some reason botched it or decided against it. Or we have been addicted to food, clothes, or gambling and somehow managed to conquer the addiction. Saints have declared that we can only reach as high as we have been low, which does not mean that we must personally experience every addiction or even suicide, but that we have empathy with addicts and suicides. We do not have to become a drug addict to know we don't want to be one, but we must experience similar emotions before we can empathize with that particular state of consciousness.

Third Stage After Death

Theosophy indicates that in the next after-death-state the soul enters into the mental plane where it begins to assimilate the mind experiences of its life. This state is sometimes called heaven. As the soul moves from the desire state to the mind realm, it experiences personal happiness. Here the ego experiences heaven to the extent of its capabilities. Materialistic thinkers who concentrated their thoughts on the physical world may recognize the heavenly realm only vaguely, and after a sleep-like condition these souls yearn again for life on earth and soon reincarnate.

Sages from many traditions teach that those who have aspired to higher ideas experience happiness in the heavenly realm. The mental aspirations they put forth in life on earth are now fulfilled. The mind makes its own world unhampered by a physical body or emotional desires. On this plane families reunite and loving relationships continue. In the mind realm love is manifest between souls on earth and souls in heaven for love is not limited by space/time.

Fourth Stage After Death

Sages and Shamans teach that the souls that lived a spiritual life on earth, acted morally, and were conscious of a higher truth, retire to a higher plane – the realm of the soul itself. In this realm the soul assimilates the essence of its earth experiences. It does not re-experience the details, for those have been experienced in the physical, desire, and mental realms and dropped away. Only deeply important impressions of the unique individual remain. These impressions form the soul's future character. Such impressions remain in the unconscious and when the soul is ready, these impressions are brought into consciousness. Meanwhile in the higher soul realm the soul bathes in the divine light of bliss, then readies itself for rebirth on earth.

Fifth Stage After Death

According to Plato and other rebirth philosophers, when the soul is ready it selects the type of future life it needs on earth to best help it grow spiritually. Retrograde lives occur only so the soul can work on an undeveloped aspect of itself. Evolution of the soul is a spiral – the general movement is metaphorically upward. Unless the soul has reached wholeness or perfection, it feels the need to reincarnate. The imperfect soul can't remain in the divine state without feeling the need to return to the earth realm for continued experiences. Before returning to earth, the soul chooses the type of life, the family, the nation, the race, and the time of birth. Gradually these characteristics accumulate almost like a magnet gathering filings.

Some say at birth the essence of our future life flashes through the soul just as at the moment of death we recall the life just lived. What we know with certainty is our birth means enrollment into a new life experience – and the process toward wholeness continues.

Chapter Thirteen

Living the Spiritual Life

Knowing is not enough; we must apply.
Willing is not enough; we must do.

Goethe

Spiritual Aliveness

Spiritual aliveness is a new birth – a birth out of the ordinary material-oriented existence into a greater awareness of living a spiritual life. In Latin, Greek, and Hebrew, the word spirit means "life breath." Thus living the spiritual life makes us alive – really alive! The whole world is alive, say the Native Americans: the mountains breathe and plants live, as do animals and human beings. The spiritual life holds a distinctive degree of aliveness – it isn't just breathing, it is something more. Spiritual aliveness is a fullness of mind and body and soul in touch with reality. As St. Thomas Aquinas said, "Spirit means our relatedness to the totality of existing things." In other words, aliveness in the spirit is our relationship to everything.

Our calling to this deep and wonderful way of life may come to us by our own natural development – our soul has been leading us unconsciously towards the awakening of the spirit within us. Or we may have been inspired through the teachings of a religion or a philosophy. Some individuals approach aliveness suddenly, by an unexpected shocking experience such as a death in the family or of a friend. The call comes to each of us according to our needs.

In whatever way the call comes, we must answer with a strong mental determination and will power to make a commitment. If we seize the moment with our mind only, our commitment will be ineffective because the truth has not only to be through ideas; the truth has to be lived daily in everything we do. Spiritual aliveness is a combination of our thoughts, our hearts, and emotions. Kierkegaard said the movement toward the spiritual life is a total commitment made by an act of will. He called this total commitment the "leap of faith."

Once we make the decision to follow the spiritual path, we may at first wander uncertainly and even lose sight of the way. But once we have made the choice, the inner guide is already at work. Whatever doubts and misgivings we have cannot triumph over the inner power that has turned the current of our life. The call, once accepted, stands. The aliveness that has been born cannot be stifled. Yes, we slip, make mistakes, fall away from the path, but these are only temporary sidesteps. The spiritual path has called and eventually we find it again. External circumstances such as a job, money, fame, and success may take us away from the spiritual pursuit, but even those obstacles cannot hold us in their power forever.

Commitment

Before we make the commitment to taking the spiritual path, we may have only an intellectual interest – an attraction towards the idea. Or we may admire someone who is devoted to the divinity, but not enough to devote ourselves to the cause. In such cases, we may need a long period of preparation. Or we may start out at a dead run and quickly lose interest. However, even these are not entirely departures from the path. Such lapses happen because there is a defect in our commitment. The mind shows an interest, the heart is attracted, the will puts forth some effort, but the whole nature has not yet given itself to the spiritual life. It has only sparked an interest and we are attracted to what might be. Some people enthusiastically experiment, but don't give themselves totally to the ideal. Yet, the effort is not lost. Though the first attempt ended up in a muddle, the preparation has been made and is therefore not wasted.

Every thought and activity that we raise from its attachment to the lower nature and dedicate to the divinity is a gain. Even one compassionate thought can remove an obstacle that opposes our progress. Our personal lives are full of bad habits, as eating junk food, listening to gossip, peeking at Tabloids, and telling little white lies. The Buddha saw our personal lives as little more than a combination of mental, nervous, and physical habits held together by our ideas, desires, and associations. It is not easy to break the habit formations of our past and create a new vision and a new way of living within. We have tried to cope with life in terms of attitudes that do not work for so long, that letting them go is one of the most difficult tasks we encounter.

Little by little, however, we exchange our surface orientation for the deeper faith and vision that sees and lives for the divine. As we change our conscious attitude, we begin to recognize that the soul is real – even more real than the external world. We begin to cease judging things as right or wrong and arguing about whether something should be done your way or my way. We begin to see every bush as a "burning bush" -- the whole world as sacred. According to Native Americans, in forgetting the sacred, we have become wounded and when we are wounded, our society is wounded, our institutions are wounded, and our planet is wounded.

To heal the wounds we need to coerce our ego nature to commit to this greater vision. We need to allow the divine to be the "alpha" or as Samuel Taylor Coleridge said, the "master of my soul." Mystics remind us that we are not called to be like Christ, but to *be* Christ. And we do this by being most truly ourselves, fully aware of what we are. But we, as everything in the world, resist change, and living the spiritual life is the most radical change we could possibly attempt. We have to throw away beliefs and attitudes and ideas that are no longer suitable – ideas about winning, about guilt, and ideas that separate secular from sacred. These old habits are obstacles to our commitment to becoming alive in the spirit. We must hold in our consciousness that we are always on sacred ground – there is no split between sacred and secular – the divinity is present everywhere.

In his book, *The Karmayogin,* Aurobindo wrote: "The Yogin sees God in all things, not only in all beings but in all events. He is the flood, He is the earthquake, He is Death that leads to a higher life, He is Pain that prepares us for higher bliss. This is a thing that cannot be argued; it has to be seen. And sight is only possible to the calm heart and the unperturbed understanding."

The point is not to convert the world, but to convert our souls to God, to see everything as the Incarnation. We would then avoid interpreting everything literally with our minds and thus go deeper into wisdom. For a while this may take us away from the world into our own quiet place where we are not available to others. From this silence we learn what our next step is, where the path is leading and how we can be of service.

In the words of Ralph Waldo Emerson, "...the sense of being which in calm hours arises, we know not how, in the soul, is not diverse from things, from space, from light, from time, from man, but one with them and proceeds obviously from the same source.... Here is the fountain of action and of thought.... We lie in the lap of immense intelligence."

Power of the Heart

The Buddha realized the power of our heart's desires. He knew the fires of our heart could tempt us in many directions. If the desires of the heart take over our lives, we are literally playing with fire. Desire or selfish craving lies in each of us and that is why the Buddha taught us to relinquish all desire. Sometimes we think relinquishing desire means we should desire nothing, want nothing, do nothing, and see nothing. But surrendering our desires does not mean giving up our job, our friends, our family and pets and escape to a cave. Relinquishing desire means a change in consciousness – to take things as they come – to let go of "I want." "I want." "I want."

When we open our hearts to the Tao, to God, Allah, the Christ, the Buddha Nature – whatever one wishes to call it –

the divine light shines through. The light softens our ego desires that carry the shadow of selfishness. This transformation is the secret power of the heart to make amends and ask forgiveness, to wean ourselves from false ambitions, and to become one with the divine. What we carry in the heart becomes not only our character, but also our destiny. The ancient Greek philosopher Heraclitus said, "Character is fate." When we change our heart, we change our destiny and become alive in the spirit.

The physical heart is the energetic source of the physical body. All other organs such as the brain, lungs, liver, stomach and kidneys are fed and cleansed by the blood pumped throughout the body by the heart. We direct the aspirations of the heart toward the divinity through love – love that flows beyond time and space and dissolves the ego. Feelings also are a function of the heart. We know when a friend or family member doesn't feel well, is angry, upset or happy. We also have feelings of goodwill and hope. When the heart is harmonious, we are able to love unconditionally. If we follow our hearts, we are given all that we need: "Ask and it will be given to you; seek, and you will find, knock, and the door will be opened to you." (Matt. 7: 7) Jean Houston wrote: "It is the closing of the heart far more than the closing of the mind that keeps folk from transformation and deepening."

Shortcuts

People have always tried shortcuts. Some monks and yogis have concentrated all their energies on the transcendent Godhead and turned away from the earth. They saw the world as evil or as illusion. The idea was to renounce the world and consecrate their higher self to God alone. But what happened to their ego nature? Was it quieted while their souls soared to the transcendent? Some aspirants killed the ego and others rejected it completely. But did they transform it? What would happen if they came out of their protected seclusion? Most of us are not in a position to give up wearing clothes or take a vow of silence. We have to continue our workaday life and follow the spiritual path spontaneously. This isn't easy, but being in the world we stay in touch with our attitudes and reactions toward people and events, thus giving us immediate insight into our ego nature. Solitude may be necessary for us along the way, but we are dependent upon food, housing, clothes, and a job, therefore we would some day have to return to the buzz of worldly life. Aurobindo found that preparation to live *in the world but be not of the world* is best made right here in the midst of things.

If we are to become whole, we need to avoid shortcuts for we have set out to conquer our ego and the world for God. When we commit to God, we commit to the highest in us – the divinity. We commit our whole selves including the physical body, emotions, and mind. Everything we are is part of the divinity. There is no doubt that life is not complete here on earth; we live in ignorance of the truth and of the transcendent Godhead, but we seek to get glimpses of the universal process. To reach our goal we willingly struggle to unveil the secret that lies within all things.

Some people explain God as a personal Father in heaven to whom we should pray and ask forgiveness. And after death we go to that place above called heaven if we are good and to a fiery underworld if we are bad. These are simple and direct answers to very complex questions. When we enter the spiritual path we are bought face to face with the extraordinary complexity of our own being. We see the stimulating and embarrassing multiplicity of our personality, the rich endless confusion of nature, and the mystery of the Absolute Reality. For those who live on the surface, life can be fairly simple. They have a small variety of desires, a few intellectual and aesthetic cravings, some tastes, a few strong ideas often disconnected, and lots of opinions. They enjoy good health and suffer disease and experience a scattering of joys and sorrows. They arrange these things in some practical fashion and call it existence. But when we plunge deep within, we find a very rich and complex subject that we want to know more about and to master.

A story about a Hindu philosophy professor beautifully describes the difference between the simple and the complex life:

A Hindu philosophy professor lived next door to a woman with no education. He watched her year after year. The woman never asked questions about her place in the universe, about the destiny of the world, or who she was at the depth of her being. She went about her daily chores in blissful ignorance. The philosopher shook his head in wonder. He had studied the complexity of the universe and taught his students the intricacies of philosophy, yet he knew he didn't know if what he was teaching was the truth. And he worried if what he taught would harm is students if it were not the truth. His neighbor had no such worries. She smiled and was happy. The philosophy professor suffered, struggled with the most difficult problems, and was not at peace.

When the professor discussed his dilemma with a friend, the friend asked him if he would like to trade places with his neighbor. The philosophy professor thought for a while then shook his head. No matter how unhappy he was, he would rather worry and struggle with the truth than go about in blissful ignorance.

Like the philosophy professor, we may ask: Would I rather be a toddler again in blissful ignorance of self and the world, or in my present state, no matter how difficult it is?

As we commit to the complexities of the spiritual path one of the most disconcerting discoveries is to find that all the parts of us – intellect, will, desires, heart, and body have their own complex nature. These parts neither agree with themselves or with each other. We discover that we are not just one but many personalities and each has its own demands and differing desires. We are a massive confusion into which we have to introduce the divine order.

Yet, as we journey, we find that we are not alone – the sharp separateness of our ego was a delusion. We are all interrelated. In the sixteenth century, St. Teresa of Avila shared her experience of this unity: "It is like rain falling from the heavens into a river or a spring: there is nothing but water there and it is impossible to divide or separate the water belonging to the river from that which fell from the heavens... Or as if in a room there were two large windows through which the light streamed in: it enters in different places but it all becomes one."

Concentration

Spiritual teachers agree that the ability to concentrate is one of the first conditions of the spiritual life. A harmonious concentration of our whole being upon the divine is an important part of the process. However, even if we commit ourselves to our aspiration toward the divine, we are too complex to open ourselves totally all at once to God. As Helen Keller said, "The truth dazzles gradually, or else the world would be blind." What we can do is set ourselves in motion and remember to ask the divinity to guide us and not submit entirely to the ego. Plato suggested that we concentrate on the rational and intuitive aspects of the soul to guide and master our emotions. As we know, unless controlled, emotions can wreak havoc. A disciplined development of goodwill allows the divine to flow into our consciousness. In one of his talks, the Dalai Lama said: "All humans want to be happy; that's universal. The path to that happiness requires discipline."

When Socrates said the most important activity for any human was to care for the soul, he meant to raise our awareness of the true and ultimate and to distinguish it from the immediate pleasures or sorrows of our worldly desires. The higher consciousness has a much greater capacity to receive the divine light than the ego, which obscures the light. With goodwill leading our heart and deepest feelings we are able to transform the ego to the divine and allow the spirit to change our lives. It is then we recognize the wisdom of

Aurobindo's words: "It is for joy and not for sorrow that the world was made."

Power of Love

We are coming closer to realizing our oneness with all living things. Science is discovering that the power of prayer can go from Australia to America and that people can communicate through their intuitive powers. The power of love can heal. As Jesus taught: "The first and great commandment is to love God with all your heart and soul and mind. The second great commandment is to love your neighbor as yourself." When we truly love, we are beyond the reach of those who are un-loving. We may receive injury from them, but we won't be offended in spirit. Thus in our love we are always happy, even in the face of slander and injustice.

"Love for yourself does not mean that you are indebted to yourself," said the Dalai Lama. "Rather, the capacity to love oneself or be kind to oneself should be based on a very fundamental fact of human existence: that we all have a natural tendency to desire happiness and avoid suffering."

Loving ourselves gives insight into our inner world and what brings us happiness. It is not a love based upon meeting our expectations. True self-love is boundless, because it is born out of freedom. When we gain insight into our inner world, we walk in fellowship with ourselves and with all beings, because our love brings us closer to their experiences of life. If people are angry we see their pain, if afraid we understand their fear. If they are happy we connect to their joy. By being in touch with these aspects of our nature, but not bound to them, we develop more empathy with others.

As we cultivate a serene mind we generate great peace, and even in our most "klutzy" moments, we still love ourselves. Serenity is the most important ingredient in our ability to concentrate. By offering the force of love, love returns to us. People know they can trust us – we won't deceive them or harm them. Recall the story of the enlightened Buddha who took his teachings to the five ascetics who disrespected him for following a way other than theirs. The Buddha's love for the five ascetics totally dissolved their anger and they became his disciples.

Our world will become more spiritual as the people in it raise their consciousness. As the Buddha and Jesus taught, the means for attaining that state of being is through unconditional love. Without love to hold the world together, the second law of thermodynamics would take over and the world would eat itself out as acid eats out a coin. Why doesn't the world annihilate itself? Because, according to Teilhard de Chardin, within each sub-atomic particle, atom, and molecule dwells the spiritual force of love that stimulates the growth of everything in the world.

The concentration of a pure thought and will and love turned together to the infinite source is the starting point of the spiritual life. The object of our seeking is the fountain of divine light that grows within us and gives us the courage to continue under even the most adverse circumstances. Our concentration may be straight and narrow or many-sided, but the awakening touch occurs when our soul realizes the divine. The *heart* opens us to the ecstasy of God's beauty and the *will* courageously drives us toward the goal.

How many times have you said, "How is it possible to look a word up in the dictionary that I can't spell?" This question also is true for God. If we do not know the infinite, for it is impossible for our finite minds to think infinity, how could we possibly concentrate on God? The *Upanishads* answer: "Thou art That." Learn to concentrate on the presence of the divinity in you and in all that you are aware of.

Awakening to the Call

Although reading scriptures and having theological discussions help, that isn't enough. At the end of our intellectual inquiry we might know much that has been said of God, yet not really know God at all. Along with the intellect we strive toward the divine through a deep aspiration, a faith, and with love in our heart. Our aspiration is often imperfect and our faith based on quicksand rather than rock. Our love may be extinguished and need to be lit again like a torch in a windy

pass, but if the soul has been called, and if we have the slight-
est awakening to its call, the mind and heart can be its fine-
tuned instruments.

The best scenario is to have an aspiration in the heart and
idea in the mind that avoids a narrow religious outlook or
one-sided belief of God and the world. An inclusive view
would open us to the beauty of esoteric teachings in all religions that could help guide us along the path. By opening to
the divine, in which all beings move and live, we experience
the kinship of all life. The divinity is both personal and impersonal in its touch upon the soul. God is personal as the infinite Person who communicates a reflection of knowledge,
power, and love in the universe. God appears to us imper-
sonally as infinite existence, consciousness, and bliss, and
because God is the ground of all existence and energy, the
material of our being.

By surrendering to God we would realize God within and
hold dearly to the process of the divine force. According to
esoteric teachings, God is the one existence, the original and
universal ecstasy that constitutes all things and exceeds them.
God is infinite consciousness that creates all movement. God
is the one illimitable being that sustains all action and experience, whose will guides the evolution of things towards their
unrealized goal. "God is the center that is everywhere and the
circumference that is nowhere."

Saints and mystics have agreed that God is the internal joy
and love that supports the soul in all its experiences and even
the ego in its struggles until our sorrows and suffering finally
end. God is love and bliss – the lover who draws all creatures
toward the joys in life. God is the will, the invisible power
that guides nature and everything in it. These great mystics
and saints agree that this is the faith we need to begin the
spiritual life – faith is the springboard from which we "leap."
When we finally reach self-realization – the truth – our faith
becomes an eternal flame of knowledge, will, and love.

Mystics warn that we must distinguish between our true
aspirations for God, the Tao, or Brahman, and what are
merely rumblings or egoistic ramblings. When we tap the true

nature of the Tao what we can manifest is the will of the Tao, God, Brahman – the light that shines through. It takes a strong will to surrender to God – to let go of ego and let God lead. Without a strong will we may fall from the path more than once and after each fall it is more difficult to step back on the path. Without a strong will, we could and probably would continue to wander to the drumbeat of our ego. But, with the will leading us along the path, the last selfish rebellion gradually fades and a greater joy enters our lives.

As much as we would like it to, the ego cannot transform itself by its own willpower into the nature of the divine. We know only too well that ego is the "knot" that separates us from God and unselfishness. One of the strongest desires we have is looking for the rewards of our actions. Rewards could be pleasure, money, fame, position, or admiration from others. We take pride in our successes. Because ego is the heart of our bondage to the worldly life, the best it can do is to surrender its control to the soul's commitment. So long as the ego controls us, we would notice only a limited change in our nature. Spiritual teachers admonish us to control our ego impulses and to turn within. Then we would view nature as divine, creatures as divine and other people as divine in their essence. We would no longer resolve a moral problem by conventional standards. It is the divine guide in us that won't be swayed by the masses. But to find this central core of self, we need to be aware that our judgment is based on the totality of what we experience of ourselves – our essence.

Enslaved to worldly desires, we are bound to duality, tossed back and forth between good and evil, grief and joy, pleasure and pain, success and failure. The whole scenario reminds me of the Greek myth of Sisyphus condemned to push the rock up the mountain. Each time Sisyphus neared the top of the mountain and stopped to rest, the rock rolled down again. Day after day, year after year, Sisyphus repeated the task. The only way to reach freedom is to outgrow our feeling of separation and become conscious souls. Freewill is the divine will. Freedom frees us from ignorance. We would act in God and not in the ego and we would make choices by obeying the living truth and not for our personal desires. With a pure heart we would plumb the depths – to make the unknown known, to exorcise an ill-intent, to make amends and ask forgiveness, to wean ourselves from false ambitions, bodily greed, lust, or anger – to work consciously to manifest the greater aspiration of the heart aligned with the divinity.

Once grounded in the spiritual consciousness by transforming the ego, we would gradually become divine instruments and pray with St. Francis: "Lord make me an instrument of your peace…"

END

Bibliography

CHAPTER ONE: THE SEARCH

Aurobindo, Sri. *The Collected Works of Sri Aurobindo.* Sri Aurobindo Ashram, 1972. Aurobindo was one of the most profound sages of the twentieth century. The Works include all of his poetry, philosophy, psychology, political writings, literary criticism, and Yoga practices.

_____. *The Life Divine.* India Library Society, 1965. Aurobindo's philosophical magnum opus includes his view of the world, involution and evolution, and human destiny

_____. *The Synthesis of Yoga,* I and II. Sri Aurobindo Ashram, 1965. These two books on yoga are masterpieces of psychological insight.

Mascaro, Juan, translator. *The Dhammapada: The Path of Perfection.* Penguin Classics, 1974. A classic version of Buddhist wisdom and practice.

Plato. *The Collected Dialogues of Plato.* Edited by E. Hamilton and H. Cairns. Bollingen Series 71. Princeton University Press, 1963. All of Plato's dialogues and letters in a single volume.

_____. *The Republic of Plato.* Translated by Francis M. Cornford. Oxford University Press, 1974. An excellent translation of Plato's philosophy, psychology, and politics.

Richards, Myra (The Mother). *Conversations.* Sri Aurobindo Ashram, 1966. A beautiful question and answer guide for living the spiritual life.

Rumi, Jelaluddin. *The Essential Rumi.* Translated by Coleman Barks and John Moyne. HarperSanFrancisco, 1995. Rumi is one of the most popular poets in the world today, seven centuries after his death. One of his most famous sayings is: "For years I knocked at God's door/and when it opened at last/I saw I was knocking from the inside."

Singer, D.W. *Giordano Bruno, His Life and Thought.* New York, 1950. A scholarly look into Bruno's life and philosophy.

The New American Bible. St. Joseph Edition. Catholic Book Publishing Co. 1970.

Thoreau, Henry David. *Walden, or Life in the Woods.* Compiled by Emory Elliot, Linda Kerber, A. Walton Litz, and Terence Martin in *American Literature.* Prentice Hall, 1991. Thoreau informs us that material possessions are burdens and bids us to simplify life to reach "self-discovery."

CHAPTER TWO: EGO AND THE ROLES WE PLAY

Armstrong, Karen. *Buddha.* HarperSanFrancisco, 2001. A beautifully written poetic account of Buddha's life and teaching.

Aurobindo, Sri. *The Synthesis of Yoga,* Vol. I. Sri Aurobindo Ashram, 1955. Part Two: "The Release from the Ego," An enlightening explanation of how we could move from egoism into divine nature.

Campbell, Joseph. *The Hero with a Thousand Faces.* 2nd ed. Princeton University Press, 1968. This is one of Joseph Campbell's best-known books and for years it has influenced seekers for self-knowledge.

Edinger, Edward F. *Ego and Archetype*. Penguin Books, 1973. An outstanding book conveying the levels of consciousness and the process of individuation.

Fordham, Frieda. *An Introduction to Jung's Psychology*. Penguin Books, 1966. This book is an excellent introduction to Jung's thought on a variety of subjects including psychological types, archetypes, and the unconscious.

Freud, Sigmund. *The Standard Complete Works of Sigmund Freud*. Edited by J. Strachey, 21 vols. Hogarth, 1955-61. Freud, known as the "Father of psychology," is one of the great revolutionaries of modern life. These volumes include his thoughts on a myriad of subjects, including art, religion, psychology, and history.

Iyer, Raghavan. *The Moral and Political Thought of Mahatma Gandhi*. New York, 1973. An insightful book on Gandhi's inner moral code.

James, William. *The Varieties of Religious Experience*. New York: Mentor Books, 1958. A highly influential study of mysticism and the relations between belief and transcendent knowing.

Ramakrishna, Sri. *The Gospel of Sri Ramakrishna*. Translated by Swami Nikhilananda. Ramarishna-Vivekananda Center, 1977. Spiritual conversations between Ramakrishna and his disciples and visitors between the years 1882 and 1886.

Wolf, Laibl. *Practical Kabbalah: A Guide to Jewish Wisdom for Everyday Life*. Three Rivers Press, 1999. Rabbi Wolf's work presents complex concepts of the Kabbalah in a way that they are easily understood.

CHAPTER THREE: THE BALANCE WITHIN

Evans-Wentz, W.Y. *The Tibetan Book of the Dead*. Oxford University Press, 1960. A Tibetan manual to guide the soul at death through the *bardos,* or "middle worlds," between this life and liberation. Evans-Wentz's introduction adds clarity and depth to our understanding.

Grant, Robert M. with Freedman, David Noel. *The Secret Sayings of Jesus: According to the Gospel of Thomas.* Great Britain: Collins Press, 1970. This gospel provides us with a good deal of insight into the ways in which early Christians and Gnostics understood the teaching of Jesus.

Lao-Tzu. *Tao Te Ching: A New English Version.* Translated by Stephen Mitchell, HarperCollins, 1992. A beautiful translation of Lao Tzu's classic manual on the art of living.

_____. *Tao Te Ching: The Definitive Edition.* Translated by Jonathan Star. Tarcher/Putnam, 2001. Star gives the first translation of each character in the *Tao Te Ching,* a tremendous help for Western readers to understand its deepest meaning.

Singer, June. *Androgyny: Toward a New Theory of Sexuality.* Anchor Press/Doubleday, 1977. Singer deals with the harmonious coexistence of masculinity and femininity within a single individual.

The New American Bible. St. Joseph Edition. The Catholic Book Publishing Co, 1970.

Wilhelm, Richard, translator: *The Secret of the Golden Flower.* Commentary by C.G Jung. Harcourt, Brace & World, New York, 1962. A book on Chinese esoteric thought indicating humans and the cosmos obey the same laws. Humans are microcosms of the universal macrocosm.

Woodman, Marion. *Addiction to Perfection.* Inner City Books, 1982. In this book Woodman maintains that many of us work so hard to create our own perfection that we forget we are human beings. Only through love can we transform ourselves.

CHAPTER FOUR: TRAINING FOR THE SPIRITUAL LIFE

Hanh, Thich Nhat. *The Heart of the Buddha's Teaching: Transforming Suffering into Peace, Joy, & Liberation.* Broadway, 1999. A beautiful and poetic introduction to the teaching of Buddhism, including the Four Noble Truths, the Noble Eightfold Path, and various sutras.

Richards, Myra (the Mother). *Words of Long Ago.* Sri Aurobindo Ashram, 1952. A small book of questions and answers on living the spiritual life.

_____. *Conversations.* Sri Aurobindo Ashram, 1966. This small book is another excellent practical guide to living the spiritual life.

Aurobindo, Sri. *The Synthesis of Yoga.* Vol. I. This book contains the four steps necessary to train for the spiritual life, plus chapters on Bhakti yoga, Jnana yoga, Karma yoga, Raja yoga, and Aurobindo's synthesis: Integral Yoga.

Aurobindo, translator. *The Gita.* Edited by Anilbaran Roy. Sri Aurobindo Ashram, 1963. Sri Aurobindo's beautiful translation of the Bhagavad Gita, which includes notes compiled from his book, *Essays on the Gita.*

Jacobi, Jolande. *The Psychology of C.G. Jung.* Forward by Dr. Jung. Yale University Press, 1973. This is an insightful work including Jung's structure of the psyche and the laws of the psychic processes and forces.

Plato. *The Republic of Plato.* Translated by Francis M. Cornford. In his "Allegory of the Cave," Plato describes the human journey from ignorance to knowledge.

The New American Bible. St. Joseph Edition, Catholic Book Pub. Co. 1970.

CHAPTER FIVE: JOURNEY OF THE SOUL

Augustine. *City of God.* Translated by Marcus Dods. Encyclopedia Britannica, 1990. The great medieval scholar and mystic wrote about the two cities: the City of God – those who love God, and the City of the World – those who love material things. Augustine was one of the most influential philosophers of the Middle Ages.

Cleary, Thomas, translator. *The Essential Confucius.* HarperCollins, 1992. This introduction to the core teachings of the great Chinese sage, philosopher, and educator provides a solid philosophical and historical background, as well as commentaries by Confucius.

_____. Translator. *The Essential Koran: The Heart of Islam.* HarperCollins, 1994. This book provides a clear and readable introduction to the Muslim scripture revealed to the Holy Prophet Mohammad.

Eckhart, Meister. *The Essential Sermons, Commentaries, Treatises, and Defense.* Translated by E. Colledge and B. McGinn. Paulist Press, 1981. Considered one of Christianity's greatest mystics, Eckhart has influenced philosophers, theologians, and mystics the world over.

Fox, Matthew. *Creativity: Where the Divine and Human Meet.* Tarcher/Putman, 2002. Matthew Fox explores the powerful connection between creativity and communicating with the Divine.

Kant, Immanuel. *Critique of Practical Reason.* Translated. by T.K. Abbott. Longmans & Greene, 1927. A very difficult read by one of the most important philosophers in the Western world. This book contains Kant's ethical writings.

Kaufmann, Walter. *Nietzsche: Philosopher, Psychologist, Antichrist.* Vintage Books, 1974. A beautifully written overview of Nietzsche's works.

Kierkegaard, Soren. *Fear and Trembling,* Translated by W. Lowrie. Princeton, 1941. A scholarly and informative book on the necessity of the "will" in making decisions.

Koller, John M. *Oriental Philosophies.* Charles Scribner's Sons, 1970. A well-written, understandable look into the Asian mind and its concern to maintain and improve human existence. An excellent discussion of Buddhism.

Lao-Tzu. *Tao Te Ching: A New English Version.* Translated by Stephen Mitchell. HarperCollins, 1992. An extremely worthwhile translation of Lao Tzu's classic manual on the art of living.

Plato. *The Republic of Plato.* Translated.by Francis M. Cornford. Oxford University Press, 1974. Plato has Socrates and friends converse about the three aspects of the soul: rational, spirited, and appetites.

_____. *Symposium.* Translated by Benjamin Jowett. Oxford University Press, 1963. This classic dialogue explores love from the different points of view: mythically, comically, poetically, philosophically, and last mystically by Plato's mentor Socrates.

Radhakrishnan, Sarvepalli and Moore, Charles, editors. *A Sourcebook in Indian Philosophy.* "The Chandogya Upanishad." Princeton University Press, 1971. An outstanding book that provides Western readers with basic source material on Indian philosophy.

Teilhard De Chardin, Pierre. *The Phenomenon of Man.* Harper & Row, 1959. A Jesuit paleontologist, Chardin joined scientific expertise and spiritual intuition in a vision of the world's evolution. He conceived creation as an ongoing process.

Wilber, Ken. *Spectrum of Consciousness.* The Theosophical Publishing House, 1977. This book provides a "bold and well documented plea to the world to recognize our basic consciousness as a state of at-one-ment."

CHAPTER SIX: WHAT GOES AROUND COMES AROUND (KARMA)

Aurobindo, Sri. *Essays on the Gita.* Sri Aurobindo Library, Inc. 1950. Insightful essays on *The Bhagavad Gita*, by one of the greatest sages of the Twentieth Century.

_____. *The Life Divine.* India Library Society, 1965. A masterful and comprehensive philosophy of the universe, human nature and human destiny.

Blavatsky, H.P. *The Secret Doctrine.* The Theosophical Publishing Co. 1888. This book is the synthesis of science, religion, and philosophy found hidden in the scriptures of the Asiatic and early European religions. It also shows the occult side of nature that has never been approached by modern civilization. Volume One: Cosmogenesis. Volume Two: Anthropogenesis.

Kant, Immanuel. *Critique of Pure Reason.* Translated. by N.K. Smith. Macmillan, 1968. One of the milestone books of Western philosophy, in which the great German philosopher argued that we cannot directly know the "thing-in-itself" (essence of things) because our minds are limited to the phenomenal world of our experience.

Epictetus. *The Art of Living: The Classic Manual on Virtue, Happiness, and Effectiveness.* A New Interpretation by Sharon Lebell. HarperSanFrancisco, 1998. Epictetus, once a slave turned great Stoic philosopher, is one of the great Stoic philosophers of the Hellenistic period.

The New American Bible. St. Joseph Edition. Catholic Book Pub. Co., 1970. (Matt. 7:12).

CHAPTER SEVEN: REINCARNATION

Aurobindo, Sri. *The Life Divine.* India Library Society, 1965. A beautiful explanation of the rebirth process and how it integrates with the Divine and the World.

Stevenson, Dr. Ian. *Reincarnation and Biology.* 2 vols. Praeger, 1997. A report of Stevenson's monumental research on memories of reincarnation reported by children, and his discoveries regarding lives that correspond to them. Fascinating case studies.

CHAPTER EIGHT: CREATION? EVOLUTION? OR BOTH?

Aurobindo, Sri. *The Life Divine.* India Society Library, 1965. A superb explanation of involution and evolution – the Divine descent and the ascent of matter. Aurobindo explains the role of the involution and evolution in our inner search for higher consciousness.

Grifiths, Bede. *The Cosmic Revelation: The Hindu Way to God.* Templegate Publishers, 1983. This book is a record of transcribed tapes based on Father Bede's talks at Conception Abbey, Missouri. Father Bede was a Catholic monk who spent much of his life in India and was deeply influenced by its spiritual traditions.

Kant, Immanuel. *The Critique of Pure Reason.* Translated by N.K. Smith. Macmillan, 1968. Kant explains the categories of the mind and alludes to the lenses we wear in our perception of the world.

Smith, Huston. *The World's Religions.* HarperSanFrancisco, 1991. In print for more than forty years, this elegant book has introduced countless people to the major religions of the world.

Teilhard De Chardin, Pierre. *The Phenomenon of Man.* Harper & Row, 1959. For Chardin, the world evolves through stages: Cosmogenesis (matter), Biogenesis (life), Noogenesis (mind), and Christogenesis (spirit). We are presently in the Noogenesis stage. Our next giant step is into the Christogenesis stage through unconditional love.

CHAPTER NINE: HIGHER CONSCIOUSNESS

Aurobindo, Sri. *The Collected Works of Sri Aurobindo.* Sri Aruobindo Ashram, 1972. These include all of Aurobindo's poetry, and his many books, articles, and letters about philosophy, psychology, political events, literary criticism, and the varieties of transformation practices.

Bohm, David. *Wholeness and the Implicate Order.* Routledge, 1973. A leading figure in quantum theory, David Bohm developed a view of physics that treats the totality of existence, including matter and consciousness, as an unbroken whole.

Bergson, Henri. *Two Sources of Morality and Religion.* Doubleday & Company, 1935. Bergson proposed two sources of morality: open morality and closed morality. Open morality and religion give us freedom based on autonomy and intuition (dynamic). Closed morality and religion are systematic and limited, based on intellect (static).

James, William. *The Varieties of Religious Experience.* New York: Mentor Books, 1958. A study of mysticism, religious conversion, and the relations between belief and transcendent knowing, by a highly influential American philosopher.

Plato. *The Republic of Plato.* Edited by Francis M. Cornford. Oxford University Press, 1974. For Plato, the physical world is an "appearance" of reality: the Forms--truth, beauty, goodness. The good individual will turn from desiring physical pleasures to seeking knowledge of the "Form of the Good" or God.

Pribram, Karl. *Perceiving, Acting, and Knowing.* Edited by R.E. Shaw and J. Bransford. Erlbaum/John Wiley, 1977. Karl Pribram's synthesis of the holographic brain model and view of the physical universe. During his researches, Pribram found that a unity characterizes the basic order of the universe.

Whitman, Walt. *Leaves of Grass.* Signet, 2000. Ralph Waldo Emerson proclaimed Whitman's life and work to be "...the most extraordinary piece of wit and wisdom that America has yet contributed."

CHAPTER TEN: RELIGION AND SPIRITUALITY

Smith, Huston. *The World's Religions.* HarperSanFrancisco, 1991. Smith has a great gift for getting eloquently to the heart of each religious tradition.

Jung, C.G. *Memories, Dreams, Reflections.* Translated by Richard and Clara Winston. Random House, 1961. Jung's autobiography, as told to his secretary, Aniela Jaffe, is a remarkable introduction to his inner world, including a collection of dreams, premonitions, synchronicities, alchemical investigations, and his midlife soul crisis.

Wilhelm, Richard, translator. *The Secret of the Golden Flower.* Harcourt, Brace & World, 1962. A book of Chinese yoga and analytical psychology, which explains the secret of the powers of growth latent in the psyche. This book gives insight into the yin/yang and the 7-fold nature of all human beings.

Govinda, Lama. *The Way of the White Cloud: A Buddhist Pilgrim in Tibet.* Shambhala, 1970. Written by a famous convert to Buddhism. Govinda first joined the Theraveda school of Buddhism, but later found his home in the Tibetan tradition. This is his account of his spiritual adventurous travels in Tibet and India.

Emerson, Ralph Waldo. *The Best of Ralph Waldo Emerson.* Walter J. Black, Inc., 1969. Emerson was deeply influenced by India's great scripture the Bhagavad Gita. With Henry David Thoreau, he is America's most famous Transcendentalist philosopher, known worldwide for his belief in self-reliance and the "over-soul."

CHAPTER ELEVEN: HOW FREE ARE WE?

Aurobindo, Sri. *The Life Divine.* India Society Library, 1965. Throughout this book, Sri Aurobindo discusses ignorance, which is a lack of freedom, and knowledge of the Divine, which frees us from the limitations of ignorance. In his small book, *Man, Slave or Free?* Aurobindo also discusses freedom and determinism.

Jung, C.G. *Psychological Reflections.* Edited by Jolande Jacobi. The Bollingen Library: Harper & Brothers, 1961. This anthology of Jung's writings includes a section on "Problems of Self-Realization," which explains why we should change internally.

Richards, Myra (the Mother) and Sri Aurobindo. *Fate and Free-will.* Compiled by Vijay from the writings of Sri Aurobindo and the Mother. Sri Aurobindo Society, 1997. Interesting and helpful writings concerning fate and freewill.

CHAPTER TWELVE: AFTER DEATH—THEN WHAT?

Aurobindo, Sri, and Myra Richards (the Mother). *Death.* Compiled by Vijay from the writings of Sri Aruodindo and the Mother. Sri Aurobindo Society, 1997. Writings about death and what happens after death. An excellent source describing the necessity of death and rebirth.

Ellwood, Robert. *Theosophy.* The Theosophical Publishing House, 1986. An excellent introduction to theosophy, the universe, the human experience, and theosophical views of life after death.

Kubler-Ross, Elisabeth. *On Death and Dying.* Collier, 1970. In this book Dr. Kubler-Ross introduces the idea of the five stages in our typical dealing with death. She also explores how imminent death affects the patient, the family, and the professionals attending the patient.

Moody, Richard. *Life After Life: The Investigation of a Phenome-*

non—Survival of Bodily Death. Mockingbird Books, 1975. Dr. Moody presents his pioneering study of more than one hundred people who experienced clinical death and were revived. These inspiring accounts give us a glimpse of the "other side" and descriptions of the unconditional love and peace that awaits us.

Plato. *The Republic of Plato*. Translated by Francis M. Cornford. Oxford University Press, 1974. In his "Myth of Er," Plato describes the fate of the soul before birth and after death. "It was indeed, said ER, a sight worth seeing, how the souls severally chose their lives—a sight to move pity and laughter and astonishment; for the choice was mostly governed by the habits of their former life."

Rinpoche, Guru, according to Kkarma Lingpa. *The Tibetan Book of the Dead: The Great Liberation Through Hearing in the Bardo*. Translation with commentary by Francesca Fremantle and Chogyam Trungpa. Shambhala, 1975. An ancient Tibetan manual for dying, which provides instruction to those attending the dying person for the soul's guidance in the realms beyond death.

CHAPTER THIRTEEN: LIVING THE SPIRITUAL LIFE

Aquinas, Saint Thomas. *Basic Writings of St. Thomas Aquinas*. Edited by A.C. Pegis, 2 vols. Random House, 1947-48. An excellent collection of the writings of the great Christian theologian and philosopher of the late Medieval Ages.

Aurobindo, Sri. *The Ideal of The Karmayogin*. Sri Aurobindo Ashram, 1966. Aurobindo explains how the spiritual life finds its most powerful expression in the person who lives the ordinary life. By living in the world we can develop a union of the inner life and the outer life.

Emerson, Ralph Waldo. *The Essays of Ralph Waldo Emerson*. The Heritage Club, 1959. Essays by the great American transcendentalist philosopher, including subjects of love, friendship, and "the oversoul" for an account of identity with the Divine.

Kierkegaard, Soren. Translated by W. Lowie. *Fear and Trembling..* Princeton, 1941 Kierkegaard takes us through life's stages: Aesthetic, Ethical, Religious (The Leap of Faith), and describes how we move from the lower to the higher stages through fear and trembling by an act of will.

Teresa of Avila, Saint. Translated and edited by E. Allison Peers. *The Interior Castle.* Image, 1961. This book is a spiritual classic of Western Christian mysticism with profound insights into the "labyrinth of the soul."

The Dalai Lama. *Ethics for the New Millennium.* Riverhead Books: Penguin/Putnam, 1999. His Holiness the Dalai Lama is the spiritual and temporal leader of the Tibetan people. In 1989 he won the Nobel Peace Prize. This book is an example of his philosophy of peace from a great reverence for all living things. According to the Dalai Lama, "human nature is basically gentle, not aggressive. And every one of us has a responsibility to act as if all our thought, words, and deeds matter."